# THE SUNDAY TIMES
# COOKBOOK

## BY SUE LAWRENCE

For Georgie + Jim,
Best wishes,

Sue Lawrence

9/10/98

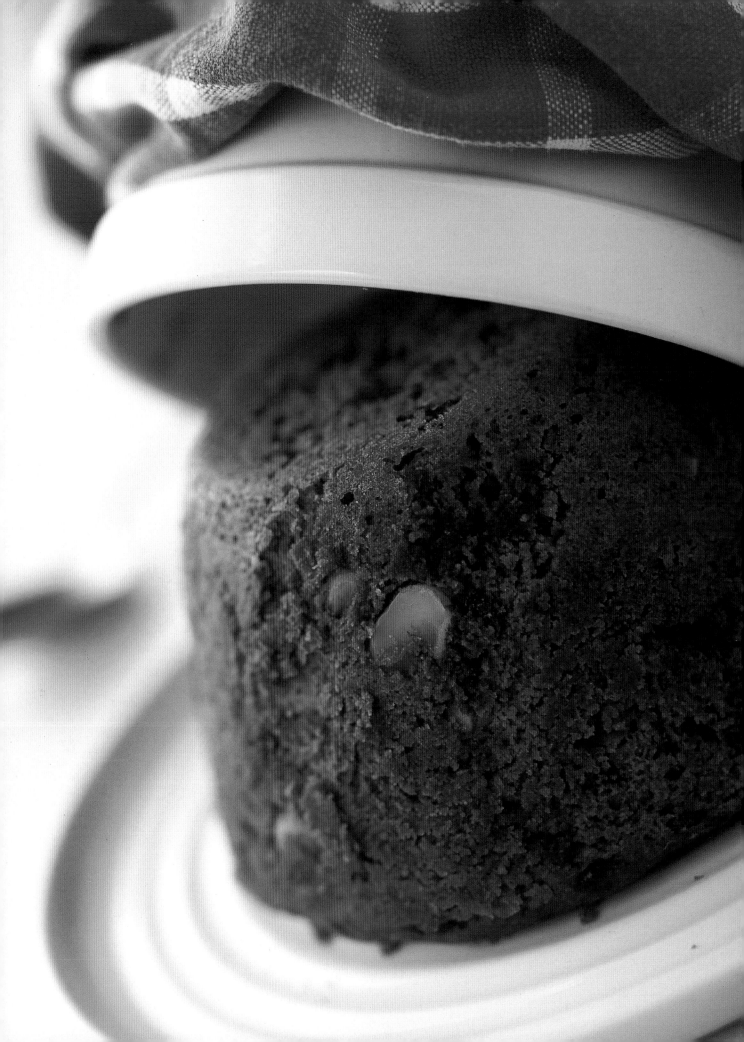

# THE SUNDAY TIMES
# COOKBOOK

## BY SUE LAWRENCE

### WINE TIPS FROM JOANNA SIMON

HarperCollins*Publishers*

# DEDICATION

For Euan, Faith and Jessica.

# ACKNOWLEDGEMENTS

Special thanks to Rachel, Jeremy, Lucas and Robert
at 'Style' for their continuing support.
Thanks also to Mary my agent, to Jane for editing this book
and to Jean and Marie-Ange for the photography.

## WINE NOTES

**Joanna Simon**, who has written the wine notes to accompany the menus
in the book, is the award-winning Wine Writer of *The Sunday Times*. Through her
articles and books she aims to bring the pleasures of wine to a new generation of
consumers and to expand the horizons of those already committed to the vine.
A former editor of both *Wine* and *Wine & Spirit International* magazines,
she has written two books (*Discovering Wine*, 1994, and *Wine with Food*, 1996).

Text © Sue Lawrence 1998
Photographs © HarperCollins*Publishers* 1998
All rights reserved

Editor: Jane Middleton
Photographs and styling: Jean Cazals
Food styling: Marie-Ange Lapierre
Indexer: Susan Bosanko

Sue Lawrence reserves the right to be
identified as the author of this work

A catalogue record for this book is
available from the British Library

ISBN 0 00 414046 X

Colour reproduction by Colourscan, Singapore
Printed and bound by Rotolito Lombarda SpA, Milan, Italy

FRONT COVER: Partridge with wild mushroom sauce (page 151)

# introduction

**M**y culinary experiences began in France. During my year out from university as *assistante* in a French school, my gustatory horizons widened beyond recognition. Having been brought up on good, wholesome Scottish fare, and in a country where food was more to fuel than to thrill (the old Presbyterian ethics die hard), it was a shock to the system to find that people talked about food incessantly. There was the shopping, the preparation, the cooking and the eating – all of these lasting far longer than I had ever experienced. I used to love watching people prodding, feeling and smelling fruit and vegetables to find the best. No expense seemed to be spared and even family meals involved only top-quality ingredients, all of which were bought daily. Men and women talked for hours about recipes and particular regional specialities, and about which wines suited them. By the time my year was up, I had become fluent not only in French but also in 'table French'. I too could talk about how the best myrtilles were to be found on certain foothills of the Pyrenees. I was familiar with six different ways to cook rabbit. I could discuss at length whether to cook the vegetables for ratatouille separately or in one pan. I knew which type of bread to accompany oysters – and which type of wine to wash them down.

But it had not always been thus. I have, of course, always loved eating with a passion, from my time guzzling chocolate pudding in a highchair (as the old photos

reveal), through student days when midnight hunger pangs would see me at the all-night bakery for warm rolls, to family Sunday lunches with a choice of custard, ice-cream or cream with the steamed pud: I always had all three. But a love of food relies on more than innate greed. A sense of adventure also helps. I'm sure I am not the only person who urges my fellow diners in a restaurant to order something different so that I can lean over with my fork and sample it. And, when travelling abroad, I try to avoid the now ubiquitous pizzas and burgers and opt for something with a genuinely local flavour.

I have been fortunate enough to travel to some wonderful places. I shall always remember sitting in a sago-palm-thatched hut in the Solomon Islands eating fish stew and coconut scones cooked by an octogenarian called Mary, whose only means of cooking was a fire, sheets of sacking and some hot stones. I have sat in the middle of a frozen lake in Lapland fishing through the ice, munching reindeer and lingonberry sandwiches. I have stood looking up at the Great Wall of China, slurping down delicious noodles that a hawker had just rustled up from a pile of flour and a jug of water. On the other hand, I have also trawled the streets of Caracas seeking something typically local only to end up rather ignominiously in a well-known hamburger joint after rampant hunger finally overcame that intrepid sense of adventure. Well, no one is perfect.

My return home from France did not herald the end of my food passion. *Au contraire*, I started cooking with a vengeance, with, of course, many notable disasters sprinkled among the successes: I too have hurled the entire contents of a dish in the bin and set off resolutely for the fish and chip shop. Some years later, once my youngest child had begun nursery school – allowing me more free time to cook – I entered and won BBC Television's Masterchef competition, which led to a career as a writer. In 1993 I was extremely fortunate to be asked to write occasional articles for *The Sunday Times*. By 1996 I had become their regular food writer, and this book – a combination of updated published recipes and a whole batch of new ones – came to be.

Because my weekly column contains an entire menu I have suggested various menus throughout this book, which is also punctuated with tips and (I hope) useful hints. The reason for writing this book is to share many favourite recipes, which have been tried and retried, so that you too might enjoy that deep feeling of satisfaction that only delicious food can bring. With so many readers bemoaning the fact that they had to rip out the recipe pages each week, it seemed to make sense to publish the most popular in one comprehensive volume – and to add to these a hundred new ones.

The recipes are exceedingly simple and use ingredients that are, hopefully,

available to everyone. Some are quick, others more time-consuming, but the fundamental theme that I hope runs through all the recipes is summed up by 'the yum factor'. If the dish tastes yummy and the post-prandial feeling is one of blissful contentment, then you can feel you have succeeded as a cook; you might even allow yourself a brief moment of smugness. As for the visual side, I confess I am not one of those cooks who put great store by the beauty of the finished dish: if it looks good, of course, it is a bonus. But the main point is that home-cooking should taste divine. From the simplest plate of scrambled eggs for breakfast in bed to a splendid dinner of roast lamb and tarte Tatin for friends, it should be food fit for the gods – delectable, luscious and memorable.

# contents

10   **starters**

24   **soups**

38   **salads**

52   **breakfasts and brunches**

64   **snacks and lunches**

82   **after-work suppers**

98   **picnics and barbecues**

112   **cooking for friends**

134   **dinners and parties**

156   **puddings**

180   **cakes and bakes**

190   **index**

**W**hen I worked as a waitress during my university holidays in the mid-1970s the choice of starters in our local restaurant was simple: prawn cocktail, soup of the day or pâté. And this was by no means unique; throughout the land, these three starters headed virtually every bill of fare, with some more sophisticated establishments perhaps opting for smoked salmon or even oysters in season.

In their own way, there was nothing much wrong with these dishes. Home-made soup is always delicious, the pâté was rich and creamy and the prawn cocktail pink and succulent, presuming the chef had remembered to defrost the prawns in time. But these days no chef worth his or her salt would put only these rather mundane dishes on the menu. For starters are there to titillate, excite and stimulate the palate. Whether for a dinner party at home or a special meal in a restaurant the starter should arouse comment – preferably oohs and aahs rather than yuk, there's too much ketchup in the Marie Rose sauce. Variety is the key to a successful starter. The prelude to a main course should remain uppermost in the mind long after the steamed pudding dish has been scraped clean. Whet your appetite on the following ...

# CHAPTER ONE
# starters

# Scallop ceviche

**SERVES 4**

6 large fresh scallops

2 tablespoons lime juice

3 plum tomatoes, skinned and diced

1 large avocado, peeled, stoned and diced

4 spring onions, finely chopped

2 tablespoons finely chopped fresh coriander

1 tablespoon extra virgin olive oil

1 tablespoon freshly squeezed orange juice

salt and freshly ground black pepper

lettuce and blue corn chips, to serve

**It is essential to use extremely fresh (never frozen) scallops for this South American-inspired dish. Serve with some blue corn chips – and a refreshing margarita or two.**

Slice each scallop thinly into about 4 pieces (remove the orangey-pink coral if you prefer). Place in a non-metallic bowl with the lime juice. Stir gently and leave to marinate for 25–30 minutes at room temperature. In a separate bowl, combine the tomatoes, avocado, spring onions, coriander, oil and orange juice and season with plenty of salt and pepper.

Drain the liquid from the scallops and discard. Add the scallops to the tomato and avocado mixture and turn gently, taking care not to break them up. Arrange a bed of lettuce in a shallow bowl, then tip the scallop mixture on top. (You can now keep this, loosely covered, at room temperature for about 1 hour.) To serve, offer a bowl of blue corn chips.

# Stir-fried squid with lemongrass

**SERVES 4**

300g/10½oz cleaned squid

3 fresh lemongrass stalks

2 tablespoons sunflower oil

3 garlic cloves, chopped

4 spring onions, chopped

1 teaspoon freshly grated root ginger

½–1 tablespoon chilli sauce

1 tablespoon light soy sauce

1 tablespoon Thai fish sauce (*nam pla*)

3 tablespoons chopped fresh coriander

**If your fishmonger has not prepared the squid for you it is easy to do yourself. Just pull out the head (and attached innards) from the body sac. Cut off and keep the tentacles but discard the rest. Then pull out the pen or quill (backbone), slip off and discard the thin membrane around the body sac and wash the squid thoroughly under running water.**

**Although it is not exactly authentic, I love to serve this stir-fry with warm flatbread to dunk into those lovely lemongrass juices.**

Cut the body of the squid into slices 1cm/½in thick and set aside with the tentacles. Remove and discard the outer layers of the lemongrass and chop the inner stalks finely.

Heat the oil in a wok (or large frying pan) until very hot. Add the lemongrass and garlic and fry, stirring, for half a minute. Add the spring onions and ginger and continue frying, stirring all the time, for 2 minutes. Add the squid and fry for another minute, then add the chilli sauce (start with ½ tablespoon, then taste for 'heat'), soy and fish sauce and, stirring well, continue to cook for another minute. Stir in the coriander, then taste for seasoning and serve at once in warm bowls.

# Spinach and goat's cheese soufflé

**The base mixture for this soufflé can be prepared several hours in advance, then the whisked egg whites folded in just before cooking. If you prefer, use individual ramekins and reduce the cooking time by about 10 minutes.**

Heat 50g/1¾oz of the butter in a saucepan, then add the flour. Stir well and cook gently to form a roux: about 2 minutes. Gradually pour in the milk, whisking constantly, and cook over a low heat until it thickens – about 3 minutes – then remove from the heat. Add the egg yolks, one at a time, beating well, then stir in the cheese.

Melt the remaining butter in a small pan, add the spinach and cook gently for 2 minutes, then drain and squeeze thoroughly dry. Transfer the spinach to a board and chop. Pat dry again with kitchen paper. Add the spinach to the sauce and season with salt and pepper. (Now you can cover the sauce tightly and chill for several hours if convenient. If it thickens when cool, warm it slightly before mixing in the egg whites.)

Whisk the 4 egg whites until stiff but not dry, then fold a quarter of these into the sauce to loosen it. Fold in the remaining egg whites very gently. Pour the mixture into a buttered 1.2 litre/2 pint soufflé dish and bake in the centre of an oven preheated to 190°C/375°F/Gas Mark 5 for 30–35 minutes or until well risen and golden brown. Serve at once.

Be sure to wipe all around the rim of the soufflé dish once the mixture has been poured in; any spillage will inhibit even rising.

## SERVES 4

65g/2½oz butter

40g/1½oz plain flour

300ml/10fl oz milk

3 medium eggs, separated, plus 1 extra egg white

125g/4½oz medium-soft goat's cheese, chopped

200g/7oz fresh spinach

salt and freshly ground black pepper

# Smoked venison with melon

**SERVES 4**

1 ripe Galia, Canteloupe or Charentais melon

175g/6oz thinly sliced cold-smoked venison

juice of ½ lemon

1–1½ tablespoons extra virgin olive oil

25g/1oz Parmesan shavings (shaved with a potato peeler)

**This is a simple plate of cold-smoked venison with juicy melon and Parmesan shavings. It is also good made with fresh figs instead of melon. My Italian friend Anna always warms fresh figs very slightly in the oven before serving as a starter, to bring out their flavour. It really works.**

Cut the melon in half and scoop out the seeds, then slice it into 8 wedges. Lay 2 of these on each serving plate and arrange the venison around it.

Squeeze the lemon juice over the melon, then drizzle the oil over the venison. Top with the Parmesan shavings and serve with warm fresh bread.

| A quick midweek supper | | Joanna's wine notes |
|---|---|---|
| Smoked venison with melon | | Dry Oloroso sherry with smoked venison is a marriage made in heaven, and dry Amontillado nearly as perfect. Both could also partner the spicy noodles but, if you prefer wine, try a Riesling (good German Kabinett or Australian), or a young, soft, medium-bodied red, served cool (e.g. Chilean Merlot, Argentinian Bonarda, or inexpensive Vin de Pays). |
| Hawker's spicy noodles | 94 | |
| Bramble clafoutis | 168 | |

# Pasta with lemon and cream

**SERVES 4**

250g/9oz fettuccine or tagliatelle

150ml/5fl oz double cream

zest of 1 large unwaxed lemon

3 tablespoons freshly grated Parmesan cheese

salt and freshly ground black pepper

**This unbelievably simple recipe is exquisitely delicious. You can use either fresh or dried pasta. I find that ribbon shapes such as fettuccine or tagliatelle work best.**

Cook the pasta in a large pan of boiling salted water until *al dente* and then drain. Meanwhile, gently heat the cream and lemon zest in a large saucepan until hot and thick, then season with plenty of salt and pepper.

Drain the pasta and toss immediately into the sauce. Add the Parmesan, toss briefly and serve in warm bowls.

# Prawns with lemongrass mayo

**SERVES 4**

2 tablespoons olive oil

2 garlic cloves, peeled but left whole

16 large (tiger/king) raw prawns, shelled and deveined

salt and freshly ground black pepper

**For the mayonnaise:**

2 plump fresh lemongrass stalks

2 medium free-range egg yolks

½ teaspoon Dijon mustard

lemon juice

150ml/5fl oz sunflower oil

150ml/5fl oz olive oil

**Serve the bowl of mayonnaise in the middle of the table to dip the warm, juicy prawns into. No cutlery is required, only fingers ... so don't forget the napkins.**

For the mayonnaise, remove the outer layers of the lemongrass and chop the inner stalks finely. Put the lemongrass, egg yolks, mustard and 1 teaspoon of lemon juice in a food processor and season with salt and pepper. Process for a few seconds, then very slowly dribble in the oil – literally drop by drop. Once you can see that an emulsion has formed, increase the oil to a thin stream and continue pouring steadily and slowly. Taste and add salt and pepper accordingly, plus more lemon juice if necessary, then tip into a bowl. Beat in ½ tablespoon of boiling water if the mayonnaise is too thick.

For the prawns, heat the oil in a frying pan, add the whole garlic cloves and cook for 2–3 minutes, until beginning to colour. Remove the garlic from the pan with a slotted spoon, then increase the heat. Add the prawns and cook for 3–4 minutes, turning once, until pink. Season with salt and pepper and then serve with the mayonnaise. Offer some warm fresh bread on the side.

# Aubergine and goat's cheese rolls

**SERVES 6**

2 large aubergines

olive oil

150g/5½ oz goat's cheese

250g/9oz ricotta cheese

4 tablespoons chopped fresh mint

black olive tapenade (bought is fine)

salt and freshly ground black pepper

**These aubergine rolls also make excellent picnic fare, served plain without the tapenade dressing.**

Using a sharp knife, cut the aubergines lengthways into slices 1cm/½in thick: you should have about 12 slices altogether. Place on an oiled grill pan and brush well with olive oil. Season with salt and pepper and grill for about 8 minutes, turning once, until golden brown and tender. Leave to cool.

Mash together the goat's cheese, ricotta and mint, adding some salt and pepper to taste.

To assemble, choose the best-looking side of each aubergine slice for the outside, then spread the other side with a thin smear of tapenade. Put a dessertspoonful of the cheese mixture on the narrow end of each slice, then roll up, carefully enclosing the filling. Chill for at least 6 hours.

To serve, bring the aubergine rolls to room temperature. Thin down 1 tablespoon of tapenade with the same amount of olive oil to give a pouring consistency. Place 2 rolls on each serving plate and drizzle over some zigzags of tapenade.

# Slow-roasted tomatoes with Parmesan, olives and capers

**You can use these roasted tomatoes in many other dishes: toss them into pasta and salads, whizz them into soups, layer them in a sandwich or picnic loaves such as the Provençal *pan bagnat*. Purée them with fresh basil or oregano to make a simple, thick sauce to accompany grilled meats or gamey fish such as tuna or red mullet.**

**Serve this starter with plenty of fresh baguette.**

Place the tomatoes on a baking sheet, cut-side up (try to pack them in tightly so they do not collapse when they soften). Sprinkle with salt, pepper and the sugar. Drizzle with 2 tablespoons of the olive oil. Place in an oven preheated to 220°C/425°F/Gas Mark 7 and cook for 20 minutes, then reduce the temperature to 150°C/300°F/Gas Mark 2 and cook for a further 1½ hours or until the tomatoes are soft and caramelized around the edges. Leave on the baking sheet to cool.

To serve, place 2 tomato halves on each plate. Mix the olives and capers together and pile them on top. Place 2 more tomato halves on top, then sprinkle some Parmesan shavings over. Whisk together the balsamic vinegar, the remaining olive oil and some salt and pepper and drizzle this dressing around the tomatoes.

**SERVES 4**

8 large plum tomatoes, halved

½ teaspoon sugar

5 tablespoons olive oil

2 tablespoons chopped black olives

1 tablespoon capers

Parmesan shavings (see below)

1 tablespoon balsamic vinegar

salt and freshly ground black pepper

To shave Parmesan, run a swivel-headed potato peeler down a whole block. And never throw away the Parmesan rind; add it to soups such as minestrones, broths or bean soups for real depth of flavour.

# Oysters with guacamole

**If you can find them, use native oysters for this recipe as they have a more distinctive taste and firmer texture. The almost-as-splendid Pacific oysters are available all year round. Ask your fishmonger to open the oysters and leave them in the half-shell.**

Remove the oysters from their shells. Halve, stone and peel the avocado. Mash it with the onion and lemon juice, then season with salt, pepper and Tabasco or chilli sauce.

Place a dessertspoonful of this mixture in the deep part of the oyster shells. Top with the oysters and serve at once, with buttered brown bread.

**SERVES 2–3**

12 oysters in the half-shell

1 ripe avocado

1 tablespoon very finely chopped onion

juice of 1 lemon

a dash of Tabasco or chilli sauce

salt and freshly ground black pepper

# Roasted ratatouille vinaigrette

**Instead of cooking this dish in plain olive oil you could make your own herb oil, which gives a much stronger flavour. The best herbs to use are rosemary, thyme, bay and oregano. Wash and thoroughly dry 5 or 6 thick sprigs of your chosen herb, place in a bottle or jar and top up with extra virgin olive oil. Add 1 teaspoon of white wine vinegar and seal the bottle tightly. Place the bottle on a windowsill and give it a good shake whenever you pass. After 10–14 days, strain the oil into a clean bottle, pop in a couple of fresh long sprigs of the herb and seal. Use the oil to toss with pasta, to roast joints of meat or to baste barbecued or grilled food.**

Place the first 6 ingredients in 2 oiled roasting tins (or use a grill pan if you own only one roasting tin). Pour over 3 tablespoons of oil and season with salt and pepper. Strew some herb sprigs over the top and roast in an oven preheated to 240°C/475°F/Gas Mark 9 for about 35 minutes or until the vegetables are golden brown and tender.

Make a dressing by shaking together 3 tablespoons of oil with the vinegar and plenty of salt and pepper. Finely chop 1 tablespoon of herb leaves from some fresh sprigs and add to the dressing. Transfer the vegetables to a shallow dish and pour the dressing over, tossing gently. Serve at room temperature, with crusty bread.

## SERVES 6

| |
| --- |
| 400g/14oz large courgettes, cut into thick rounds |
| 2 large aubergines, cut into thick rounds |
| 1 large red pepper, deseeded and cut into thick slivers |
| 4 garlic cloves, peeled but left whole |
| 1 large red onion, peeled and cut into eighths |
| 2 large tomatoes, cut into eighths |
| 6 tablespoons olive oil (or herb oil – see introduction) |
| sprigs of fresh thyme, rosemary or oregano |
| 1 tablespoon sherry vinegar |
| salt and freshly ground black pepper |

# Turkish aubergine dip with garlic and dill

**This is wonderful spread on toasted pitta bread or used as a dip for raw vegetables. It is important to squeeze out the aubergine flesh really well, otherwise the dip will be runny.**

Put the aubergine and garlic cloves on a baking tray and place in an oven preheated to 230°C/450°F/Gas Mark 8 for 15 minutes. Remove the garlic and continue cooking the aubergine for 10 minutes or until it feels soft and the skin is charred and black.

Snip off the ends of the garlic cloves and squeeze out the soft insides into a food processor. Once the aubergine is cool enough to handle, remove the skin and scrape out the soft flesh. Squeeze thoroughly dry in your hands – or between kitchen paper. Place the aubergine flesh in the food processor and add the lemon juice, yoghurt, dill and oil. Whizz until smooth, then add salt and pepper to taste (you will need quite a lot of salt).

Spoon into a bowl and chill for a couple of hours. Serve with toasted or warmed Turkish *pide* or Greek pitta bread.

## SERVES 4

| |
| --- |
| 1 large aubergine |
| 3 large garlic cloves, unpeeled |
| juice of 1 lemon |
| 2 tablespoons Greek yoghurt |
| 2 tablespoons chopped fresh dill |
| 1 tablespoon olive oil |
| salt and freshly ground black pepper |
| pitta bread, to serve |

# Grilled aubergines with sweet chilli paste

## SERVES 6

2 large aubergines

3 tablespoons olive oil

salt and freshly ground black pepper

**For the chilli paste:**

2 tablespoons olive oil

2 large onions, finely sliced into rings

4 red chillies, halved, deseeded and finely sliced

1 teaspoon allspice

zest of 1 lemon

200g/7oz molasses sugar

100ml/3½fl oz water

200ml/7fl oz red wine vinegar

**Although the aubergines must be grilled at the last minute, the sweet chilli paste can be made several days in advance and stored somewhere cool. If you have any left over it is very good served with grilled or barbecued meats.**

For the chilli paste, heat the oil in a pan and add the onions. Fry gently for 10 minutes, until softened, then add the chillies and cook for 2 minutes. Add the remaining ingredients, stir well and bring slowly to the boil. Once the sugar has dissolved, increase the heat to medium and cook, uncovered, for about 35 minutes or until the mixture is dark, sticky and fairly thick. Most of the liquid will have evaporated. Stir frequently or the paste will burn. Spoon into a bowl and leave until cold, then cover and keep somewhere cool.

Remove and discard the aubergine stalks, then cut each aubergine lengthways into 3 thick slices. Score the flesh on each side to form a crisscross pattern. Rub the olive oil into each side and season liberally with salt and pepper.

Place the aubergines on a sheet of foil on a grill pan and grill for 10 minutes, turning once, until golden brown and tender. Remove and leave to cool for 5–10 minutes. Serve warm, with a small amount of the chilli paste spread over the top.

# Stilton and pear salad

## SERVES 4

1 tablespoon cider vinegar

4 tablespoons olive oil

½ teaspoon Dijon mustard

a selection of watercress, young spinach and lettuce leaves

2 ripe pears

75g/2¾oz Stilton, crumbled

salt and freshly ground black pepper

**This is an ideal way of using up all those leftover pieces of Stilton after Christmas. Roquefort also works well.**

Whisk together the vinegar, oil and mustard and season with salt and pepper. Place the salad leaves in a large bowl. Toss in three-quarters of the dressing.

Halve and core (but do not peel) the pears and cut them into thin slices. Arrange on top of the salad, then top with the cheese. Pour over the remaining dressing and serve with bread.

# Pacific ceviche

**SERVES 6**

500g/1lb 2oz very fresh fish (swordfish is best; cod, rock turbot and scallops are also good)

4 limes

150ml/5fl oz coconut milk (from a can)

½–1 red chilli, deseeded and chopped

2 teaspoons freshly grated root ginger

½ teaspoon salt

salad leaves, to serve

1 tablespoon fresh coriander leaves

freshly ground black pepper

**This recipe is based on a dish I ate in a friendly yet decidedly ramshackle hotel situated on a beach in the stunningly beautiful Solomon Islands. I had travelled there to do a story on tuna fishing. After 24 hours of eating raw tuna at sea (5 minutes out of the water), prepared sashimi-style by the Japanese bosun, I was ready for a change. This coconut-milk ceviche was on the menu that night and I found it a delicious way of treating fish. As with any marinated raw fish dish, use only the freshest fish. If in doubt about its freshness, make another recipe instead.**

Cut the fish into thin slices and place in a non-metallic bowl. Squeeze over the juice of 3 of the limes, cover and leave for about 45–50 minutes, stirring gently half way through.

Place the coconut milk, chilli, ginger and salt in a bowl. Grind in plenty of black pepper and stir. Drain and discard the liquid from the fish and add the fish to the coconut milk mixture, with the juice of the remaining lime. Stir gently and leave for at least 1 hour, but no more than 3 hours.

To serve, place the salad leaves in a bowl and pour over the fish and marinade. Tear over the coriander leaves and serve with bread.

# Goat's cheese, thyme and black olive gratin

**SERVES 4**

1 large tomato, cut into 4 thick slices

300g/10½oz soft goat's cheese

1 tablespoon fresh thyme leaves

1 heaped tablespoon Greek yoghurt

100g/3½oz black olives, stoned

salt and freshly ground black pepper

**This starter can be whizzed together in a couple of minutes, then grilled until hot and bubbling. Serve it with plenty of crusty bread, to spread the goat's cheese mixture on.**

Put the tomato slices on kitchen paper and pat dry. Place the cheese, thyme and yoghurt in a food processor, add plenty of salt and pepper and process briefly, until smooth.

To assemble, put the tomato slices in a 20cm/8in gratin dish. Top with the olives, then spoon over the cheese mixture, smoothing the top. Place under a preheated grill for about 4–5 minutes, until bubbling and tinged with golden brown. Serve at once and eat spread on to bread.

# Asparagus with herb mayo, toasted hazelnuts and Parmesan

**This divine combination makes a wonderful starter for any spring menu. You can use whichever herbs you have to hand but chervil, tarragon, basil and dill are particularly good. If you have never made mayonnaise before, be sure that the eggs are at room temperature and that you add the oil literally drop by drop at first, then in a slow, steady drizzle. Any leftover mayonnaise can be stored in the refrigerator for a few days, as a dip for crudités (or, if you are feeling decadent, chips).**

For the mayonnaise, place the egg yolks, mustard, lemon juice and plenty of salt and pepper in a food processor and process for a few seconds. Then slowly dribble in the oil, drop by drop. Once an emulsion has formed, increase the oil to a thin stream. Tip the mayonnaise into a bowl (beating in ½ tablespoon of boiling water if you find it too thick). Stir in the chopped herbs and check the seasoning.

Cook the asparagus in boiling water for 5–8 minutes or until just tender. Drain well and pat dry. Place on 4 serving plates. Spoon a dollop of mayonnaise to one side and scatter over the nuts and cheese. Serve at once, while the asparagus is still warm.

## SERVES 4

500–600g/1lb 2oz–1lb 5oz asparagus, trimmed

25g/1oz toasted hazelnuts, roughly chopped

25g/1oz Parmesan shavings (shaved with a potato peeler)

**For the mayonnaise:**

2 medium free-range egg yolks

½ teaspoon Dijon mustard

1 teaspoon lemon juice

300ml/10fl oz oil (I like to use half sunflower, half olive)

2 tablespoons chopped mixed fresh herbs

salt and freshly ground black pepper

If your mayonnaise curdles, do not hurl the whole lot. Just whisk in a teaspoon of very cold water or a whole ice cube and it should soon recover its glossy, creamy texture.

**S**oup played a very important role in my childhood. There was always a soup pot on the go, whatever the weather, and there was always soup on offer for unexpected visitors. If there were more guests than soup, something else was thrown into the pan to eke it out. On the whole, it was hearty broths, lentil and split pea soups. We ate soup at home every day before the main course and my friends did too, as I discovered when I went to their houses for tea. It was not something to be talked about, as we would talk about how Mrs Grieve always made the best chips, Mrs Doig's meatroll was so moreish and Mrs Marwick's cherry pie to die for; soup was just there, to be eaten and to nourish.

When I spent my year in Finland I was amazed that the Finns were not more of a soup-eating nation, since it was such a cold country. My amazement abated on Thursdays, however. In the part of Finland where I lived, Thursday meant one thing: pea soup. Everyone ate thick, hearty pea soup with a dollop of mustard for lunch. To follow there was a baked pancake served with a topping of lingonberry jam. Thursdays never failed to delight during my months in the frozen north, and often now I try to recreate that meal, served with a puffy jam pancake for pudding. But I confess, I am not quite as dogmatic about which day of the week it is served.

# CHAPTER TWO

# soups

# Cauliflower cheese soup

**SERVES 4**

40g/1½oz butter

1 onion, chopped

1 large potato, peeled and chopped

1 medium cauliflower, cut into florets

1.2 litres/2 pints hot chicken stock

225g/8oz Bonchester or Cooleeny cheese

salt and freshly ground black pepper

chopped fresh chives, to garnish

**You can use Camembert or Brie for this soup but since we have such splendid farmhouse cheeses in Britain and Ireland nowadays I like to use either a Bonchester or a Cooleeny – both Camembert-style cheeses made from cow's milk in the Scottish Borders and County Tipperary, Ireland respectively.**

Heat the butter in a large saucepan and gently fry the onion and potato for about 10 minutes, until softened. Add the cauliflower florets, stirring to coat them with the butter. Season with salt and pepper and add the hot stock. Bring to the boil, then cover, lower the heat and simmer for about 20 minutes or until the vegetables are tender. Liquidize the soup in a blender (in batches) and return to the saucepan.

Remove and discard the rind of the cheese, then chop up the cheese. Place in a bowl with 2 ladlefuls of the hot soup. Stir to melt the cheese, then pour the mixture back into the saucepan. Reheat the soup, stirring continuously, until piping hot but do not allow it to boil. Serve in warm soup bowls, garnished with a sprinkling of chopped chives.

Leftover cauliflower cheese can be converted into soup: just heat it up with chicken stock, a few fresh herbs and some single cream. Whizz in a blender and serve with a swirl of cream, some chopped chives and grated Cheddar.

# Roasted red pepper soup

**SERVES 6**

600g/1lb 5oz red peppers

1 tablespoon olive oil

1 onion, chopped

2 garlic cloves, chopped

2 celery sticks, chopped

1 tablespoon tomato purée

900ml/1½ pints hot chicken stock

salt and freshly ground black pepper

soured cream or smetana, to serve

**If you prefer, cook the peppers in an oven preheated to 180°C/350°F/ Gas Mark 4 for at least 30 minutes instead of grilling them.**

Cut the peppers into quarters and remove the seeds. Place the peppers on a sheet of foil under a hot grill until the skins are charred and blackened. Remove from the grill, wrap in the foil and leave for about 15 minutes, then peel off the skins and chop the flesh.

Heat the oil in a frying pan and gently fry the onion, garlic and celery for 5 minutes. Add the peppers and fry for a further 3 minutes, then add the tomato purée and hot stock. Bring to the boil, cover and simmer for about 10 minutes. Blend or liquidize, then season and reheat if necessary. To serve, swirl a spoonful of soured cream or smetana into each bowl of soup.

# Salmon and sorrel soup

When cooked, sorrel tends to turn sludgy brown very quickly. If you make it into a pesto, however, it retains its lively green colour and sharp, almost lemony flavour. Here the pesto is served with a fresh salmon soup based on one I ate in Lapland made with local salmon.

Use any leftover sorrel pesto in pasta dishes, or mix it with mayonnaise and some crème fraîche and serve with cold poached salmon.

For the pesto, place the sorrel, pine nuts, Parmesan and garlic in a food processor and process briefly until the sorrel is chopped. Slowly add the oil through the feeder tube and process until the mixture becomes a thick paste. (Alternatively, you can do all this by hand using a pestle and mortar.) Season to taste and set aside.

For the soup, place the potatoes and stock in a saucepan and bring to the boil. Cook for about 10 minutes or until the potatoes are almost tender. Stir in the leek, peppercorns and plenty of salt. Place the salmon chunks on top, then cover and simmer for 10–12 minutes over a low heat until the fish is just cooked. Do not stir or the fish will break up.

To serve, taste the soup and adjust the seasoning. Ladle into warmed soup bowls, then top each portion with about ½ tablespoon of the pesto. Offer extra pesto in a bowl at the table.

### SERVES 4

| |
|---|
| 600g/1lb 5oz potatoes (peeled weight), diced |
| 900ml/1½ pints fish stock |
| 1 large leek, thinly sliced |
| 10 black peppercorns |
| 500g/1lb 2oz fresh salmon (tail-end fillet is fine), skinned and cut into large chunks |
| salt and freshly ground black pepper |

**For the sorrel pesto:**

| |
|---|
| 200g/7oz young sorrel leaves, stalks removed |
| 3 tablespoons pine nuts, toasted |
| 2 tablespoons freshly grated Parmesan cheese |
| 2 garlic cloves, crushed |
| 100–125ml/3½–4fl oz extra virgin olive oil |

# Creamed mushroom soup with soy

This lovely creamy soup has a wonderfully elusive flavour which comes from the addition of soy sauce. I like to use chestnut mushrooms but button mushrooms are fine. It is extremely important to keep tasting this soup as you reheat it, for some soy sauces are saltier than others. You can shake in a couple of dashes of extra soy at the table if you wish.

Heat the butter in a large pan, add the onion and garlic and cook gently for about 10 minutes, until softened. Add the mushrooms and cook for 5 minutes, stirring. Add the sage leaves and hot stock, bring to the boil, then cover, reduce to a simmer and cook for about 15 minutes.

Whizz the soup in a liquidizer and tip back into a saucepan. Stir in the cream, soy sauce and some salt and pepper to taste. Reheat until piping hot, then serve.

Add a few shakes of soy sauce to any mushroom dish; use dark soy to make your dish strongly flavoured, light soy for a more delicate finish.

### SERVES 6

| |
|---|
| 50g/1¾oz butter |
| 1 onion, chopped |
| 3 garlic cloves, chopped |
| 750g/1lb 10oz mushrooms, chopped |
| 4–5 fresh sage leaves, torn |
| 1 litre/1¾ pints hot chicken (or vegetable) stock |
| 150ml/5fl oz double cream |
| 2 tablespoons light soy sauce |
| salt and freshly ground black pepper |

# Gazpacho with prawns

## SERVES 4

750g/1lb 10oz ripe tomatoes, skinned, deseeded and chopped

1 red pepper, chopped

1 red onion, chopped

2 garlic cloves, chopped

½ cucumber, peeled and chopped

1 tablespoon fresh basil leaves

1 tablespoon fresh flat-leaf parsley

1 tablespoon balsamic vinegar

200ml/7fl oz tomato passata

2–3 drops of Tabasco sauce

3 tablespoons extra virgin olive oil

200g/7oz cooked tiger prawns, peeled

salt and freshly ground black pepper

4 fresh basil sprigs, to garnish

**This is not an authentic Andalusian gazpacho, which is based on bread as well as a multitude of vegetables. Mine is simply a mixture of ripe tomatoes, red pepper, cucumber, red onion and herbs, blended, chilled and served with tiger prawns. Of course, you could garnish it with the usual gazpacho toppings – croûtons, chopped olives, hard-boiled eggs – for a change.**

Pat the tomatoes dry on kitchen paper, then put them in a blender with all the remaining ingredients except the oil, prawns, seasoning and basil sprigs (unless you have a very large blender you will need to do this in 2 batches). Add 2 tablespoons of the olive oil and process for a couple of minutes, until blended but still slightly chunky. Taste and add salt and pepper accordingly. Pour into a bowl and chill for at least 6 hours, until really cold.

An hour or so before serving, toss the prawns in the remaining olive oil and season with salt and pepper. To serve, check the seasoning of the gazpacho, then ladle it into 4 chilled soup bowls. Place a spoonful of prawns in the middle and a sprig of basil on top.

# Fish in Asian broth

## SERVES 4

2 tablespoons olive oil

1 large leek, sliced

2 garlic cloves, chopped

1 thick fresh lemongrass stalk (or 2 thin ones)

1 red chilli, deseeded and finely chopped

2 teaspoons freshly grated root ginger

900ml/1½ pints fish stock

1 tablespoon Thai fish sauce (*nam pla*)

600g/1lb 5oz monkfish or cod fillet, cut into thick chunks

2 tablespoons chopped fresh coriander

**Be sure to use fresh-looking lemongrass or you will not be able to chop it finely enough. And only use young ginger, otherwise you will have too many fibres – blue-tinged ginger flesh is a sign that it is old.**

Heat the oil in a saucepan and gently fry the leek and garlic for about 10 minutes. Meanwhile, remove the outer layers of the lemongrass and chop the inner stalks finely. Add the lemongrass, chilli and ginger to the pan and fry for about 3 minutes. Add the fish stock and fish sauce and bring to the boil. Cover and simmer for about 10 minutes, then add the chunks of fish. Cook gently for 4–5 minutes or until the fish is just done. Stir in the coriander, taste for seasoning and serve at once.

# Lentil and ginger soup

**SERVES 8**

25g/1oz butter

1 onion, chopped

2 celery sticks, chopped

3 garlic cloves, chopped

2 heaped teaspoons freshly grated root ginger

350g/12oz orange lentils, well rinsed

1 bay leaf

1.4 litres/2¼ pints hot chicken (or vegetable) stock

salt and freshly ground black pepper

**This lovely soup is based on Indian dal, which I always enjoy when it is heavy on the ginger. Add a small spoonful of cumin seeds for extra spiciness, if you like.**

Heat the butter in a large saucepan and add the onion, celery, garlic and ginger. Cook gently for 10–15 minutes, until softened, then add the lentils, bay leaf and hot stock. Bring to the boil, then cover, reduce the heat and simmer for about 30 minutes. Take out the bay leaf, liquidize the soup until smooth and season to taste with salt and pepper. Serve piping hot, with warmed naan bread.

# Chilled avocado soup with chilli jam

**SERVES 6**

50g/1¾oz butter

1 onion, finely chopped

2 garlic cloves, finely chopped

1 celery stick, chopped

1.2 litres/2 pints chicken stock

4 ripe avocados, peeled, stoned and chopped

3 heaped tablespoons Greek yoghurt

juice of 1 large lemon

salt

**For the chilli jam:**

150g/5½oz red chillies, deseeded and chopped

150g/5½oz onions, thinly sliced

150g/5½oz granulated sugar

1 lemon, cut into quarters

100ml/3½fl oz water

**Although this soup should be made on the day of serving, the chilli jam can be cooked several days in advance.**

Melt the butter over a low heat and stir in the onion, garlic and celery. Fry gently for about 10 minutes, then add half the stock. Cook for about 20 minutes, stirring occasionally, then remove from the heat and leave to cool. Place in a blender with the avocados, remaining stock, yoghurt and lemon juice: you will need to do this in batches. Process until smooth, then add salt to taste. Pour into a bowl, cover and chill for 1–2 hours.

For the jam, put all the ingredients into a saucepan and bring slowly to the boil. Cook, uncovered, for 20–30 minutes, until thick and sticky, then remove from the heat and discard the lemon quarters. Leave to cool.

To serve, ladle the soup into chilled soup bowls and top each portion with a spoonful of the chilli jam.

# Parsnip soup with Arbroath smokies

**This is a thick, wintry soup topped with flaked Arbroath smokies and a drizzle of olive oil. It not only looks yummy it tastes wonderful, with the sweetish, faintly smoky taste of parsnips complementing the smoky flavour of the fish so well. Hot-smoked haddock – or smokie, as it is called in Scotland – can be eaten cold (it is already fully cooked) or used in tarts, mousses, pancake fillings or soups. If you cannot find Arbroath smokies, use ordinary smoked haddock, but if it is a cold-smoked fillet you will need to cook it briefly before flaking.**

Heat the oil in a large saucepan and gently fry the onion, garlic and celery for about 10 minutes. Add the parsnips and cook for 5 minutes, stirring to coat them with the oil. Add the hot stock and some salt and pepper and bring to the boil. Cover, reduce to a simmer and cook for about 25 minutes or until the vegetables are tender. Liquidize in a blender with the sherry and taste for seasoning. The resulting soup should be fairly thick but if you find it too thick, just add a little boiling water and whizz again.

To serve, ladle the soup into 4 warmed soup bowls. Top with the flaked smokies, then drizzle over some extra virgin olive oil. Serve at once.

To remove the flesh easily from an Arbroath smokie, warm it briefly in foil in a low oven (or in a microwave, without foil). Then press down, inside the fish, all along the backbone with your thumb to release the flesh from the bone.

## SERVES 4

2 tablespoons olive oil

1 onion, chopped

2 garlic cloves, chopped

3 celery sticks, chopped

750g/1lb 10oz parsnips, chopped

750ml/1¼ pints hot chicken stock

100ml/3½fl oz dry sherry (or Noilly Prat)

200g/7oz Arbroath smokie flesh (2 small smokies)

salt and freshly ground black pepper

extra virgin olive oil, to serve

# Tom yam soup

**My recipe is a variation on a northern Thai dish, which really is spicy. The name means spicy (*yam*) liquid (*tom*). Instead of chopping up the lemongrass, simply bash the stalks well to release their exotic flavour.**

Bring the stock to the boil and add the chicken breast, lemongrass stalks, garlic and half the chilli. Cover the pan and simmer for 10–15 minutes or until the chicken is cooked through.

Strain the liquid into another saucepan. Once the chicken is cool enough to handle, shred the meat and add to the pan with the spring onions, coriander and the remaining chilli. Reheat for 1 minute, then serve at once.

## SERVES 2

600ml/1 pint chicken stock

1 large chicken breast

2 fresh lemongrass stalks, bruised

2 garlic cloves, chopped

1 red chilli, chopped

3 spring onions, chopped

1 tablespoon chopped fresh coriander leaves

# Clam chowder in a sourdough breadbowl

On the Californian coastline you almost trip over diners supping chowders or chilli con carne out of made-to-measure sourdough bread bowls. Amazingly, the locals invariably leave the bowl once the soup is finished. I think that is the best part – ripping apart the chowder-soaked bread and devouring every last crumb.

If you can buy fresh clams, they are ideal for this soup. Simply put about 1.5kg/3lb 5oz well-scrubbed, tightly closed clams in a large saucepan with the wine and stock, cover and bring to the boil. Cook, shaking the pan occasionally, until the shells open – about 5 minutes. Strain the cooking liquor through muslin or several sheets of kitchen paper to remove any grit, then remove the clams from their shells. Reserve the cooking liquor to use for the soup.

Heat the butter in a large pan and fry the onion and celery for about 10 minutes, until softened and golden. Add the bacon and potatoes and fry gently for another 10 minutes, stirring. Add the wine and stock and bring to the boil. Season with salt and pepper, then reduce the heat, cover and simmer for about 15 minutes or until the potatoes are cooked. Add the drained clams – be sure to rinse tinned ones thoroughly before using – and the cream to the chowder and reheat gently until piping hot. Adjust the seasoning if necessary.

To prepare the bread bowl, cut the top off the loaf and remove the bread from inside, leaving a thick wall and base about 2.5cm/1in all round. Replace the lid, wrap loosely in foil and place in an oven preheated to 180°C/350°F/ Gas Mark 4 for about 10 minutes or until hot.

Just before serving, place the bread bowl on a large serving dish. Ladle in as much chowder as possible (any extra can be added later) and sprinkle over the parsley.

## SERVES 4

| |
|---|
| 25g/1oz butter |
| 1 onion, chopped |
| 2 celery sticks, chopped |
| 100g/3½oz unsmoked bacon, chopped |
| 200g/7oz potatoes (peeled weight), diced |
| 150ml/5fl oz dry white wine |
| 500ml/18fl oz chicken stock |
| 2 x 290g tins of clams, rinsed |
| 150ml/5fl oz double cream |
| 1 large, deep, round sourdough loaf (preferably 1 day old) |
| 1 tablespoon chopped fresh parsley |
| salt and freshly ground black pepper |

## A valentine's dinner

**Clam chowder in a sourdough bread bowl**

**Roast cod with a coconut and lime sauce and mango salsa** 146

**Cape gooseberries with double chocolate fondue** 170

## Joanna's wine notes

Valentine's Day cries out for Champagne, and the clam chowder and cod make perfect partners for a *brut* (dry) non-vintage or, if you are splashing out, a luxurious vintage Champagne. But chocolate will kill it, so, for the pudding, choose a half bottle of powerful, raisin-sweet Australian liqueur muscat or a 10-year-old tawny port.

# Grenadian spinach and coconut soup

**SERVES 6**

40g/1½oz butter

1 leek, sliced

2 garlic cloves, chopped

1 large sweet potato (preferably orange-fleshed), peeled and chopped

200g/7oz fresh spinach

1 x 200g block of coconut cream, chopped

1 litre/1¾ pints boiling water

freshly grated nutmeg

salt and freshly ground black pepper

**This is based on a soup I enjoyed on the Caribbean island of Grenada. Callaloo, a coarse, spinach-like leaf, was boiled up with sweet potatoes, corned beef and coconut milk (which is, of course, freshly grated and strained on the island). It was served with little dumplings to make a substantial dish. My soup is simply spinach, sweet potato and coconut cream, flavoured with nutmeg, which is grown all over the beautiful volcanic island.**

Heat the butter in a large saucepan and add the leek, garlic and sweet potato. Fry gently for about 10 minutes, stirring, then add 150g/5½oz of the spinach, the coconut cream and the boiling water. Season with salt, pepper and a generous grating of nutmeg and bring to the boil. Cover and simmer for about 20 minutes or until the vegetables are tender. Tip everything into a liquidizer with the remaining spinach (you will probably need to do this in batches) and blend until smooth. Season again, according to taste. Serve piping hot.

# Mushroom, lemon and noodle soup

**SERVES 4**

1 litre/1¾ pints chicken stock

zest and juice of 1 large lemon

25g/1oz butter

300g/10½oz mushrooms, thickly sliced

4 spring onions, sliced

3 garlic cloves, chopped

150g/5½oz Chinese egg noodles

1 heaped tablespoon chopped fresh chives

salt and freshly ground black pepper

**Use whichever type of mushroom you fancy for this zesty soup. Plain old button mushrooms are absolutely fine; some of the less common varieties such as shiitake or blewitts will lend a more exotic flavour.**

Bring the stock to the boil, then add the lemon zest and juice. Cover and remove from the heat. Leave to stand for at least 30 minutes.

Heat the butter in a saucepan and gently fry the mushrooms, spring onions and garlic for about 10 minutes. Then add the stock and bring to the boil. Stir in the noodles and cook for about 4 minutes or until just tender. Season with salt and pepper to taste. Stir in the chives, then ladle the soup into bowls to serve.

# Roasted pumpkin soup

SERVES 4

1 large pumpkin (about 3–4kg/
6¾–9lb)

25g/1oz butter

1 large onion, chopped

2 garlic cloves, chopped

2 large parsnips, chopped

1 heaped teaspoon ground cumin

1 heaped teaspoon ground coriander

1 litre/1¾ pints hot chicken stock

100g/3½oz young spinach

salt and freshly ground black pepper

crème fraîche and chopped fresh
chives, to garnish

**Choose a wide, dumpy pumpkin for this recipe: it is not only to be the basis of your soup, it is also your soup tureen.**

Using a sharp knife, cut the top off the pumpkin, leaving a deep base for your tureen. Scrape out all the seeds and fibrous strands with a metal spoon – or your hands. Put the pumpkin in a lightly oiled roasting tin and cover with 2 sheets of oiled foil. Place in an oven preheated to 190°C/375°F/Gas Mark 5 for about 1½ hours, until the flesh feels tender to the tip of a knife.

Meanwhile, heat the butter in a large saucepan and gently fry the onion and garlic for about 2 minutes. Add the parsnips and fry for a further 5 minutes. Add the spices and fry for 2 minutes, then stir in the stock. Cover and cook over a medium heat for about 20 minutes or until the vegetables are tender.

Once the pumpkin is cooked, drain away any liquid in the base, then carefully spoon out the flesh from the sides to leave a substantial wall about 2.5cm/1in thick. Do not scoop out the flesh from the base. You should have about 600–700g/1lb 5oz–1lb 9oz pumpkin flesh. Re-wrap the pumpkin in foil and return it to the switched-off oven to keep warm. Drain the pumpkin flesh well in a sieve, then put it in a blender (in 2 batches) with the parsnip mixture and the spinach. Whizz together until smooth and season to taste with salt and pepper.

Carefully transfer the pumpkin to a serving dish (one that will give a snug fit), using 2 wide fish slices or large spatulas. Ladle in the soup, top with a dollop of crème fraîche and some snipped chives and serve immediately.

## Autumn dinner

**Roasted pumpkin soup**

**Lamb and quince tagine**     115

**Plums in sloe gin**     160

## Joanna's wine notes

A delicious match for the soup is a spicy Gewürztraminer (most are from Alsace but look out for New World ones). The tagine, too, needs a spicy wine but red is more suitable. Try one from the Rhône, the south of France (e.g. Corbières or a Grenache) or from Portugal (but not a Daõ).

# Cabbage soup with a cheese and mustard crust

**Whenever the weather turns cold, do consider this soup. It makes a hearty, filling bowlful that will banish every last vestige of winter chill. It was inspired by a recipe from Georgeanne Brennan's lovely book, *Potager*. Her soup is made with borlotti beans and cavolo nero – that dark and interesting green vegetable that the River Café has brought from obscurity to fame – topped with an anchovy- and thyme-flavoured crust.**

Heat the oil in a deep saucepan and gently sauté the onion with the garlic and bacon until softened. Add the potato and cabbage, stir well and cook for 5 minutes. Stir in the thyme leaves and the hot stock and bring to the boil. Season with plenty of salt and pepper, then cover and simmer for about 20 minutes.

While the soup is cooking, make the crust: sift the flour and salt into a bowl and rub in the butter. Stir in the mustard and 50g/1¾oz of the cheese, then slowly pour in the milk, cutting the mixture through with the back of a knife until incorporated. Using floured hands, gather the dough together and place on a floured board. Roll out to a circle about 25cm/10in in diameter.

Check the seasoning of the soup and then ladle it into a deep ovenproof dish, about 25cm/10in in diameter. Now, using a wide spatula or 2 fish slices, quickly lift the rolled-out dough on top of the soup: either lay it across the top of the dish or lay it directly on the surface of the soup. Sprinkle the remaining cheese over the top and place immediately in an oven preheated to 220°C/425°F/Gas Mark 7 for 20–25 minutes, until the topping has risen and is golden brown and crusty.

To serve, snip off a section of crust and ladle out the soup underneath. Place the crust on top of the portion of soup.

## SERVES 4–6

1 tablespoon olive oil

1 onion, chopped

3 garlic cloves, chopped

4 smoked streaky bacon rashers, chopped

1 large potato, peeled and diced

1 small or ½ large Savoy (or green) cabbage, shredded

1–2 teaspoons fresh thyme leaves

1.2 litres/2 pints hot beef stock

salt and freshly ground black pepper

**For the crust:**

225g/8oz self-raising flour

½ teaspoon salt

75g/2¾oz butter

2 teaspoons wholegrain or Dijon mustard

75g/2¾oz mature Cheddar cheese, grated

200ml/7fl oz milk

**R**emember the days when a salad meant a tired leaf or two of lettuce, a wedge of dried-up, tasteless tomato, a grey-ringed slice of hard-boiled egg and a purple, bleeding chunk of vinegary beetroot? Oh and don't forget the squoosh of salad cream on top. The 'cold meat and salad' option simply added a slab of meat to this dreary pile.

Fast-forward a decade or two: we have now changed the whole concept of salad. It is either served in a bowl large enough to enable you to toss all the ingredients lavishly together or it is arranged in an attractive little hillock on a large dinner plate. The components have altered beyond all recognition. Fresh herbs, exotic salad leaves and tropical vegetables now vie with radicchio, romaine or Webb's lettuce. Salads are also more often served as main courses, bulked out with goat's cheese, seafood, poultry, game or meat. Accompanied by plenty of warm, fresh, crusty bread to wipe up the wonderful oily dressing on your plate, there are few simpler or more delicious dishes. Fresh, clean-tasting and revitalizing, a salad definitely comes under the category of 'looks good, tastes good – and does you good'.

# CHAPTER THREE

# salads

# Roasted pumpkin and sesame salad

## SERVES 6

1 small pumpkin (or large butternut or acorn squash)

5 tablespoons olive oil

100g/3½oz sesame seeds

1 tablespoon freshly squeezed orange juice

6 spring onions, chopped

2 tablespoons chopped fresh coriander

½–1 red chilli, deseeded and finely chopped

salt and freshly ground black pepper

**You can use either regular Cinderella-style pumpkin for this recipe or butternut or acorn squash. Serve with warmed naan bread.**

Peel the pumpkin, remove the seeds and weigh out about 800g/1lb 12oz flesh. Cut this into large chunks and put them in a roasting tin with 2 tablespoons of the oil and some salt and pepper. Turn gently to coat, then place in an oven preheated to 200°C/400°F/Gas Mark 6. Cook for about 30 minutes or until just tender to the point of a sharp knife. The pumpkin should be cooked but still firm, not mushy.

Meanwhile, dry-fry the sesame seeds (in a non-stick pan, without fat): keep shaking the pan so they do not burn. They are ready once you can smell a nutty aroma and they begin to pop. Tip on to a plate to cool.

When the pumpkin is cool enough to handle, cut it into bite-sized chunks and place in a bowl. Pour over the remaining oil and the orange juice. Turn carefully, then allow to cool until barely warm. Add the sesame seeds, spring onions, coriander and chilli. Season to taste with salt and pepper and serve barely warm or cold.

# Artichoke, rocket and Parmesan salad

## SERVES 6

90g/3¼oz rocket

280g jar of chargrilled artichokes in olive oil

110g/4oz Parmesan cheese, coarsely grated or shaved

1 tablespoon balsamic vinegar

salt and freshly ground black pepper

**The idea for this wonderful salad was given to me by Clarissa Dickson Wright. I then made it for a party of 80 guests, where it went down extremely well. The marvellous thing about it is that you can prepare it several hours in advance, then just dress it at the last minute.**

**It is important to use artichokes that have been preserved in pure olive oil, not a mixture of vegetable and olive oils, for the oil forms the salad dressing.**

Place one-third of the rocket leaves in a large salad bowl and season with salt and pepper. Chop the artichokes roughly and place half on top. Drizzle half the oil from the jar over the top. Top with half the Parmesan. Repeat the layers – rocket, artichokes, oil, Parmesan – then finish with a layer of rocket. Season generously as you go.

Cover with clingfilm and leave somewhere cool for up to 6 hours (and for at least 1 hour). Just before serving, pour over the vinegar and toss everything well with salad servers.

# Smoked haddock and parsnip salad with roasted chilli vinaigrette

**Use Anaheim, fresno or Kenyan chillies for a medium-hot flavour; habanero or Scotch bonnet for an intense heat.**

To make the chilli vinaigrette, place the chilli halves and whole peeled garlic cloves in a small ovenproof dish, pour over 1 tablespoon of the oil and roast in an oven preheated to 200°C/400°F/Gas Mark 6 for 20 minutes, turning once. Remove from the oven, snip the chillies into small pieces with kitchen scissors, then tip everything into a food processor with the remaining olive oil and the vinegar. Whizz until blended and then season to taste.

Place the haddock on an oiled grill tray (or foil if you prefer), brush with a little oil, then cook under a preheated grill for about 3 minutes. Very carefully turn the fish over, using a fish slice, and grill for a further 3 minutes or until it is just cooked.

Meanwhile, cook the parsnips in a pan of boiling salted water for 2–3 minutes or until just tender. Do not overcook. Drain, then toss with the roasted chilli vinaigrette while still warm.

Put the salad leaves in a bowl. Flake the fish into large chunks and place them on the salad leaves, then tip the parsnips and vinaigrette over the top. Toss and serve at once.

## SERVES 6

| |
|---|
| 2 red chillies, halved and deseeded |
| 2 large garlic cloves, peeled but left whole |
| 4 tablespoons olive oil, plus extra for brushing |
| 1 tablespoon sherry vinegar |
| 3 undyed smoked haddock fillets |
| 400g/14oz parsnips, cut into matchsticks |
| salt and freshly ground black pepper |
| mixed salad leaves, to serve |

# Pancetta and fig salad with hazelnut dressing

**Pancetta is an Italian belly pork similar to British streaky bacon. If you can't buy thinly sliced pancetta, use bacon instead.**

Make the dressing by mixing together the hazelnuts, oils and vinegar and seasoning with plenty of pepper and a little salt.

Fry the pancetta in a large non-stick pan over a high heat (without added fat) for 4–5 minutes, until crisp. Meanwhile, tip the spinach into a large salad bowl. Grill the fig quarters under a medium heat for about 1 minute on each side, or on a griddle pan for about 30 seconds on each side, until they are heated through.

Toss the dressing through the spinach, top with the figs, then drain the pancetta on kitchen paper and place on top. Serve at once.

## SERVES 4

| |
|---|
| 50g/1¾oz roasted hazelnuts, chopped |
| 2 tablespoons hazelnut (or walnut) oil |
| 2 tablespoons sunflower oil |
| 1 tablespoon sherry vinegar |
| 100g/3½oz pancetta slices |
| 1 large bag of baby spinach leaves |
| 4 ripe fresh figs, quartered |
| salt and freshly ground black pepper |

# Scallop salad with soy vinaigrette

**SERVES 4**

3 tablespoons rice vinegar

2 tablespoons soy sauce

1 tablespoon lemon juice

1 tablespoon sesame oil

3–4 tablespoons sunflower oil

12 plump fresh scallops

1 large bag of lamb's lettuce and rocket, washed

**Depending on what's in season, you could substitute mizuna or rocket for the lamb's lettuce.**

Make the vinaigrette by shaking together the vinegar, soy sauce, lemon juice, sesame oil and 2 tablespoons of the sunflower oil in a screw-top jar.

Pour 1 tablespoon of sunflower oil into a heavy-based frying pan and heat until very hot. Once it is searing hot (and this will take 3–5 minutes), add half the scallops (they will spit) and cook for 2–3 minutes altogether, turning them after 1 minute. Remove from the pan and keep warm. Cook the remaining scallops, using more oil if necessary.

Toss the lamb's lettuce in the soy vinaigrette, then top with the seared scallops. Serve at once, with crusty bread.

# Prawn and mint salad

**SERVES 4**

1 large head of Cos/romaine lettuce

3 tablespoons extra virgin olive oil

700g/1lb 9oz large (tiger/king) raw prawns, shelled and deveined

juice of 1 large lemon

3 heaped tablespoons chopped fresh mint

salt and freshly ground black pepper

**This warm salad should be eaten at once, before the lettuce leaves have a chance to become limp. Plenty of good French bread is essential for dunking purposes.**

Put the lettuce leaves in a large salad bowl. Heat the oil in large frying pan until very hot. Ensure the prawns are thoroughly dry, then add them to the pan and fry for about 1 minute on each side: no more than 3 minutes altogether. They are ready when their colour changes from clear to pinkish.

Mix the lemon juice and mint together in a large bowl and season with salt and pepper. Tip the prawns and the pan juices into this bowl, then tip this all over the lettuce. Serve at once.

To prepare prawns, simply peel off the thin shell; the tiny 'legs' will come away too. With a sharp knife, slit half way down the back, open out slightly and locate the intestinal tract, which is a long black thread. Scrape this out carefully with the tip of the knife, then wash the prawn under cold running water and pat thoroughly dry.

# Black bean and red pepper salad

## SERVES 6

225g/8oz black beans

3 bay leaves

1 large red pepper

3 tablespoons chopped fresh parsley

2 garlic cloves, chopped

3 tablespoons olive oil

1 tablespoon red or white wine vinegar

salt and freshly ground black pepper

**Black beans are one of South America's favourite ingredients, used especially in Brazil's fabulous national dish, *feijoada* – beans cooked with onion, chilli, smoked pork, sausages, tongue, pig's ears and trotters, and cured beef. It is served with toasted *farofa* (cassava meal) and sliced oranges.**

**Remember to start this recipe the day before, to soak the beans.**

Soak the beans overnight in cold water. Drain and rinse well, then cover in plenty of fresh cold water. Add the bay leaves and bring to the boil. Boil rapidly, uncovered, for 10 minutes, then cover and reduce to a simmer. Cook for a further 30 minutes or until tender. Drain thoroughly.

Grill the pepper until charred, then peel off the skin. Cut in half, remove the seeds and dice the flesh.

While the beans are still warm, mix in the diced pepper and all the remaining ingredients, adding plenty of salt and pepper. Taste and check the seasoning. Serve at room temperature.

---

If your recipe calls for dried beans and you don't have time to soak and cook them, use two 400g tins of beans (or chickpeas) for every 225g/8oz dried beans called for in the recipe.

---

# Butter bean and parsley salad

## SERVES 4

400g tin of butter beans

3 heaped tablespoons chopped fresh flat-leaf parsley

2 shallots, finely chopped

juice of 1 large lemon

1 large tomato, skinned and diced

1 tablespoon extra virgin olive oil

salt and freshly ground black pepper

**I think butter beans are the most comforting of beans. I can't really explain why, but perhaps it's because of their soft, floury texture and satisfyingly hearty size, combined with the fact that they were the only beans known to me in my childhood. They are certainly not as fashionable as, say, the aduki or cannellini but I just love them.**

Drain the beans well and place in a bowl with the parsley. Mix all the remaining ingredients together, seasoning generously. Add to the bowl and stir well. Leave for an hour or so before serving at room temperature.

# Steak salad

**This is an extremely tasty dish and exceedingly quick to prepare. Use only the best-quality British beef – preferably organic. Eat with plenty of warm baguette or ciabatta bread.**

Combine the oil, vinegar, spring onions, horseradish sauce and capers and season with salt and pepper.

Heat a chargrill pan (or heavy-based frying pan) and smear it with oil. Season the steaks and add them to the pan. Cook for about 4 minutes on each side (depending on thickness), until medium-rare. Meanwhile, put the watercress and rocket in a bowl.

Cut the steaks diagonally into thick slices. Toss the dressing with the salad leaves, top with the steak and serve at once.

## SERVES 4

| |
|---|
| 3 tablespoons olive oil |
| 2 tablespoons white wine vinegar |
| 2–3 spring onions, chopped |
| 1 heaped teaspoon horseradish sauce |
| 2 heaped teaspoons capers, drained |
| 2 large fillet steaks (about 200g/ 7oz each) |
| salt and freshly ground black pepper |
| watercress and rocket leaves, to serve |

## Salad days

**Scallop salad with soy vinaigrette**    42

**Steak salad**

**Warm berry compote with rose petal ice-cream**    164

## Joanna's wine notes

Wine to go with the steak salad has to cope with the piquant dressing and the meat. Try a good *cru* Beaujolais such as Fleurie, served cool, or break the mould with the intense fruitiness of a Chardonnay from New Zealand or unoaked Australian Chardonnay. If you go for Beaujolais, choose a crisp white with the scallops, e.g. Alsace Pinot Blanc or Chilean Sauvignon Blanc.

# Duck and orange salad

**You will need either 3 large or 4 medium duck breasts for this salad.**

Heat a heavy-based frying pan until very hot. Using a sharp knife, score the skin of the duck breasts, then place in the hot frying pan, skin-side down and without added fat. Cook for 2 minutes, then turn and cook for a further 2 minutes. Place on a baking tray and cook in an oven preheated to 220°C/425°F/Gas Mark 7 for 12–15 minutes, depending on the thickness. Leave to rest for about 10 minutes.

Peel the orange and cut it into thin segments, removing any pips. Place the radicchio and rocket in a large salad bowl. Mix the oil and orange juice with some salt and pepper, pour on to the salad leaves and toss well.

Once the duck has rested, cut each breast into 5 or 6 slices and place on top of the salad. Top with the orange segments and serve at once.

**SERVES 4**

| |
|---|
| 3–4 duck breasts, skin on |
| 1 large orange |
| 1 large radicchio |
| 1 large bag of rocket |
| 3 tablespoons olive oil |
| 1 tablespoon freshly squeezed orange juice |
| salt and freshly ground black pepper |

# Caesar salad

**There are many variations on this salad, and many of them are truly abominable. But the essential ingredients are Cos/romaine lettuce, croûtons, anchovies, egg, Worcestershire sauce, lime juice and Parmesan cheese. As long as you stick to these you can't go too far wrong.**

**The original Caesar salad was, of course, made by Caesar Cardini in his restaurant in Tijuana, Mexico, in 1926. The story goes that he invented it in honour of the pilots at the Rockwell Air Force base in San Diego, just over the border.**

Place the lettuce leaves in a large salad bowl: tear them up if you like; I prefer to leave them whole.

Fry the bread in a tablespoon of the olive oil until crisp, then drain on kitchen paper. Place the egg in a pan of cold water and bring slowly to the boil. Boil for 1 minute, then place in cold water. Once it is cool enough to handle, crack the egg into a food processor (scrape out all the partially cooked white, too) and add the garlic, remaining olive oil, lime juice, Worcestershire sauce and anchovies. Whiz until combined, then add black pepper to taste. You will probably not require salt.

To serve, pour the dressing over the leaves and toss well. Top with the croûtons and Parmesan.

**SERVES 2**

| |
|---|
| 12–16 large Cos/romaine lettuce leaves |
| 2 thick slices of white bread, cut into large dice |
| 4 tablespoons olive oil |
| 1 large free-range egg |
| 1 large garlic clove, crushed |
| 1 tablespoon lime juice |
| 2 teaspoons Worcestershire sauce |
| 4 anchovy fillets, mashed |
| 25g/1oz Parmesan cheese, coarsely grated |
| freshly ground black pepper |

# Thai seafood salad

SERVES 2 AS A MAIN
COURSE, 4 AS A STARTER

4 tablespoons sunflower oil

juice of 1 lime

1 tablespoon Thai fish sauce
(*nam pla*)

a pinch of sugar

1 garlic clove, crushed

½–1 red chilli, finely chopped

50g/1¾oz cleaned baby squid,
sliced

100g/3½oz large raw prawns,
shelled and deveined

100g/3½oz monkfish fillet, cut
into large chunks

salt and freshly ground black pepper

Cos/romaine lettuce, to serve

**You can use all sorts of different seafood for this provided it is firm-textured. Add extra chilli if you like a really fiery taste.**

For the dressing, put 2 tablespoons of the oil in a screw-top jar with the lime juice, fish sauce, sugar, garlic and chilli. Season with salt and pepper and shake to combine.

Heat the remaining oil in a heavy-based frying pan or wok, then add the squid, prawns and monkfish. Fry over a high heat, stirring, until done – about 3 minutes.

Chop the lettuce if the leaves are large, then place in a salad bowl. Toss the lettuce with the dressing, then remove the hot seafood from the pan with a slotted spoon and place on top of the salad. Toss and serve at once.

# Mint couscous tabbouleh

Nowadays most couscous available is precooked, so all it needs is a very short steaming time. In this recipe, it is simply 'cooked' by leaving it to stand in hot water for about 20 minutes. It is important to fork up couscous well, in order to eliminate any lumps. My French friend Sabine does this in the Moroccan way, by diving in with both hands and running the grains through her fingers.

Place the couscous in a bowl and pour over the boiling water. Fork through, then cover tightly with a doubled tea towel. Leave to stand for at least 20 minutes. Meanwhile, shake all the dressing ingredients together in a screw-top jar.

Fork through the couscous again to remove any lumps. Add the salt and the dressing. Once the couscous is cold, stir in the mint, parsley, tomatoes and cucumber. Serve in a large, shallow bowl lined with lettuce leaves.

Keep a jar of home-made vinaigrette in the refrigerator for up to 5 days and shake well before dressing your salad.

## SERVES 6

200g/7oz couscous

300ml/10fl oz boiling water

½ teaspoon salt

7–8 tablespoons chopped fresh mint

2–3 tablespoons chopped fresh flat-leaf parsley

3–4 tomatoes, skinned and chopped

½ cucumber, diced

lettuce leaves, to serve

**For the dressing:**

4 tablespoons olive oil

1 tablespoon lemon juice

1 garlic clove, crushed

salt and freshly ground black pepper

## A summer supper

**Salt- and dill-cured salmon** 142

**Herb and mustard roast chicken** 133

**Mint couscous tabbouleh**

**Nectarine and blueberry slump** 177

## Joanna's wine notes

You could drink red wine with the mustardy chicken but I would celebrate summer with white. The savoury dishes go equally well with fine German Kabinett or Alsace Riesling, or with a vibrant Chardonnay, especially a New Zealand one. Splash out on a sweet Loire (e.g. Vouvray) or a Sauternes with the pudding.

# Provençal tuna and rice salad

## SERVES 6

250g/9oz long-grain rice

1 large shallot, finely chopped

4 tablespoons extra virgin olive oil

1 tablespoon lemon juice

1 teaspoon Dijon mustard

2 plum tomatoes, diced

2 hard-boiled eggs, quartered

1 x 200g tin of tuna, drained

1 heaped tablespoon chopped fresh flat-leaf parsley

salt and freshly ground black pepper

During my stay in Arles as an au pair, I experienced many gastronomic 'firsts': my first taste of rabbit, aubergine, courgette, wild bilberries and fresh figs. The whole way of life was so different, including a very early lunch (12 noon) and a late dinner (8pm) with absolutely no sustenance in between, which was difficult for a Scot brought up on endless between-meal cups of tea with scones, pancakes or cakes.

At weekends the routine often altered, and sometimes picnics were planned. I couldn't believe the preparations for a simple family picnic. Unlike the average British picnic, where sandwiches were cut and a Thermos of coffee made up, Madame would set about roasting a whole chicken, then send her daughters to the *boulangerie* for baguettes. Fresh cheese was bought and the red wine carefully selected. One of my favourite picnic dishes was Madame's tuna and rice salad, which was truly simple but so moreish. When I make it now I always think of Provence and wish there was even a hint of those alluring aromas of lavender, rosemary and thyme in the air. I long to feel the heat of the midday sun on my skin. I shut my eyes and try to picture the charming Provençal countryside that Van Gogh fell in love with many years before.

Cook the rice in boiling salted water until fluffy, then drain. Mix together the shallot, oil, lemon juice, mustard and some salt and pepper, then pour this mixture over the warm rice. Stir well to coat. Leave to cool, then stir in the remaining ingredients. Check the seasoning and serve at room temperature.

# Bacon, avocado and papaya salad

## SERVES 4

4 tablespoons extra virgin olive oil

1 tablespoon lime juice

1 tablespoon freshly squeezed orange juice

1 large bag of young spinach

1 large papaya (pawpaw), peeled, deseeded and diced

1 large ripe avocado, peeled, stoned and diced

200g/7oz back bacon rashers

salt and freshly ground black pepper

Serve this colourful salad with some soda bread.

Prepare the dressing by shaking together the oil, lime juice and orange juice in a screw-top jar, then seasoning with salt and pepper.

Place the spinach in a large salad bowl and add the diced papaya and avocado. Grill or fry the bacon until crisp, then snip it into bite-sized pieces and add to the salad. Pour over the dressing and gently toss everything together. Serve at once.

**A**nother title for this chapter could be morning food. Call it breakfast, brunch or whatever you like, these are the things to tease you out of your soporific stupor. And even if your idea of breakfast is nothing more than a mug of strong black coffee and a couple of multivitamins, you might be tempted by some of the dishes here that are lighter on the digestion than the traditional full-fry. Preserves are also included in this chapter, as most people eat them in the morning. Since the sad demise of afternoon tea, when scones, clotted cream and jam were *de rigueur*, jam and lemon curd have slotted nicely into place alongside marmalade and honey at breakfast time.

Although it might seem a strange idea, breakfast or brunch is a wonderful time to entertain. Everyone's guard is down in the morning and absolutely nothing is expected of us. We need not flirt, sparkle or be amusing; we simply need to be there. It is, therefore, one of the most relaxed meals for entertaining. Serve copious amounts of Buck's Fizz and you will probably end up with one of the best parties ever. The only trouble is, your guests will enjoy themselves so much that they will still be there at supper time.

# CHAPTER FOUR
## breakfasts and brunches

# Bagels with lox and cream cheese

**SERVES 6**

6 fresh bagels

175–200g/6–7oz cream cheese

175–200g/6–7oz smoked salmon slices

**Optional toppings:**

skinned diced tomato

finely chopped red onion

chopped fresh chives

The classic bagel has a glossy crust and smooth surface, created by boiling the dough briefly before baking. The texture should be moist and pleasantly chewy. Kosher bakeries (and some artisan bakers) are where you will find the real thing. Any bagel not freshly made (i.e. made that morning) should be split and toasted before being filled.

Lox is the New York terminology for their salty, lightly smoked salmon.

Split each bagel in half. Spread one half generously with cream cheese and cover with smoked salmon. If you want, top with the tomato, onion and chives. Place the other half of the bagel on top and press together.

# Scrambled eggs with Parma ham

**SERVES 1**

3 medium eggs

1 tablespoon milk (or cream)

25g/1oz butter

25g/1oz Parma ham, cut into slivers

salt and freshly ground black pepper

Remember to cook scrambled eggs slowly and always underdo them slightly: they continue cooking in the heat of the saucepan even after everything has been switched off. The Parma ham adds a certain *je ne sais quoi* – the carnivore's equivalent of smoked salmon scrambled eggs. Eat with plenty of hot Granary toast.

Beat together the eggs, milk and plenty of salt and pepper. Slowly melt the butter in a saucepan over a low heat, then increase the heat to medium (not high) and add the eggs. Stirring frequently, cook for no more than 3–4 minutes, until they are just beginning to firm up. Switch off the heat, stir in the ham and stir again. Serve at once, with toast.

| A festive brunch party | | Joanna's wine notes |
|---|---|---|
| Scrambled eggs with Parma ham | | This is the time to bring on a New World sparkling wine – white or rosé. The best from Australia, California and New Zealand are made in the same way as champagne, but taste fruitier, softer and less acid – which makes them ideal for late morning drinking. They also combine well with fresh orange juice, if anyone wants Bucks fizz. |
| Bagels with lox and cream cheese | | |
| Cranberry cinnamon muffins | 61 | |
| Panettone French toast with orange-fried blueberries | 57 | |

# Warm smoked salmon, Brie and avocado croissants

**This is something I devised when, as usual, I overcatered for a dinner party and bought far too much cheese and smoked salmon. At breakfast the next morning we feasted on these rich but delicious croissants. Reblochon makes a good substitute for the Brie.**

Split each croissant horizontally, then spread one half with the cream cheese. Top with a couple of slices of smoked salmon and then the avocado. Sprinkle over some lemon juice and plenty of black pepper. Place the Brie slices on top of the avocado and put under a preheated grill for about 1 minute or until the cheese begins to melt. Place the plain croissant halves on the side of the grill pan to heat through. Remove from the grill and quickly sandwich together. Eat while still warm and gooey.

**SERVES 6**

6 large croissants

125g/4½oz cream cheese

300g/10½oz smoked salmon slices

2 large avocados, peeled, stoned and sliced

lemon juice

300g/10½oz Brie, rind removed, sliced

freshly ground black pepper

# Ham and spinach omelette

**This takes just five minutes to rustle up from start to finish. I know this only too well: how often have I rushed home late to find a starving child needing food two hours ago? For breakfast, serve with grilled tomatoes. For a late brunch, you could serve it with a salad.**

Beat the eggs in a bowl, then add the spinach and mustard. Season well with salt and pepper.

Melt the butter in an omelette pan until hot. Pour in the egg mixture and cook for 2–3 minutes until nearly set. Then lay the ham on one side and, using a large spatula, carefully fold the omelette over to enclose the ham. Cook for further 1–2 minutes, then serve at once.

**SERVES 1**

3 medium eggs

25g/1oz young spinach leaves, coarsely chopped

½ teaspoon wholegrain mustard

15g/½oz butter

1 slice of smoked ham

salt and freshly ground black pepper

# Corned beef hash

An all-American favourite, hash sometimes includes roast beef, chicken or smoked fish instead of corned beef. In New England there is a traditional recipe, red flannel hash, made with beetroot and corned beef.
   Top the hash with a poached or fried egg and a dash of Worcestershire sauce for a truly satisfying breakfast.

Boil the potatoes and parsnips whole for 10–15 minutes, until tender to the point of a knife. Drain well and pat dry. When cool, cut into 1cm/½in dice.

Heat the oil and butter in a large, heavy-based frying pan and fry the onion for about 10 minutes, until softened and golden brown. Add the potatoes and parsnips and fry over a fairly high heat for 10–15 minutes, stirring occasionally, until the base starts to become golden brown and crusty.

Season generously with salt and pepper, then stir in the corned beef. After a few minutes, add the parsley and continue cooking for 3–4 minutes, until piping hot and crusty. Taste for seasoning, then serve straight from the pan, with or without eggs.

## SERVES 6

750g/1lb 10oz potatoes, peeled

200g/7oz parsnips, peeled

2 tablespoons olive oil

25g/1oz butter

1 large onion, sliced

250g/9oz corned beef, roughly chopped

2 heaped tablespoons chopped fresh flat-leaf parsley

salt and freshly ground black pepper

# Panettone French toast with orange-fried blueberries

This recipe will thrill those who enjoy panettone bread and butter pudding, as it has the soft inners and crusty outers of the nursery pudding but takes a mere five minutes to make.

Cut the panettone slices into quarters. Whisk together the eggs, milk and caster sugar. Pour into a large bowl and add the panettone quarters. Leave to soak for about 3–4 minutes, turning, until the liquid has been absorbed.

Heat 25g/1oz of the butter in a large frying pan and, once bubbling, add 4 of the panettone pieces. Fry them over a medium heat for about 2–3 minutes on each side, until golden brown. Transfer to kitchen paper to drain and keep warm while you add another 25g/1oz butter to the pan to fry the remaining panettone.

Meanwhile, melt the remaining butter and the icing sugar in a small frying pan over a low heat. Once melted, increase the heat to medium and add the blueberries. Cook for 2–3 minutes, stirring occasionally, then remove from the heat and stir in the orange zest.

Once all the panettone is cooked, sprinkle with caster sugar and serve with the blueberries.

## SERVES 8

2 slices of panettone, about 2.5cm/1in thick (weighing about 350g/12oz in total), cut from a panettone about 18cm/7in in diameter

2 medium eggs

300ml/10fl oz full-fat milk

25g/1oz caster sugar, plus extra for sprinkling

75g/2¾oz butter

25g/1oz icing sugar

225g/8oz blueberries

zest of 1 orange

# Polenta-fried tomatoes

## SERVES 4

4 large tomatoes, thickly sliced

65g/2½oz polenta

40g/1½oz Parmesan cheese, freshly grated

3 tablespoons olive oil

salt and freshly ground black pepper

**These are good served alongside a breakfast fry-up, as a change from plain grilled tomatoes. Or serve them as a starter, on toasted ciabatta with a little extra drizzle of olive oil and a garnish of fresh herbs.**

Place the tomato slices on a couple of layers of kitchen paper and pat thoroughly dry. Mix the polenta, Parmesan and some salt and pepper together on a plate.

Heat half the oil in a frying pan until hot. Dredge half the tomato slices in the polenta mixture, pressing gently to coat on either side. Fry for 2–3 minutes on each side, until golden brown and crisp. Remove from the pan and keep warm while you coat the remaining tomatoes and fry them in the remaining oil. Serve warm.

# Granola

## MAKES ABOUT 1kg/2¼lb

200g/7oz whole shelled nuts (I use a mixture of brazils, hazelnuts, walnuts and almonds)

1 teaspoon ground mixed spice

500g/1lb 2oz jumbo oatflakes

100g/3½oz desiccated coconut

250g/9oz unsalted butter

225g/8oz runny honey

200g/7oz dried fruit (such as apricots, mango, papaya, raisins, etc.), chopped

**Serve this granola topped with some fresh fruit – sliced strawberries, bananas, brambles, blueberries – and pour over some cold milk. It's also lovely just nibbled straight from the jar. When I visit the USA I always like to start breakfast in a diner with a bowl of granola topped with blueberries, to accompany the endless cups of coffee.**

Place the nuts in a food processor with the mixed spice and 2 handfuls of the oats. Process briefly (about 10 seconds) until the nuts are roughly chopped into good-sized chunks. Do not overprocess or they will turn into an oily paste. Tip the nuts into a bowl and stir in the remaining oats and the coconut.

Melt the butter and honey together (in a saucepan or in the microwave). Pour on to the oat mixture and stir well with a wooden spoon. Lightly butter 2 swiss roll tins (about 23 x 33cm/9 x 13in) and divide the mixture between them, patting it down evenly. Place in an oven preheated to 170°C/325°F/ Gas Mark 3 for about 30 minutes or until golden brown. If you have both trays in one oven you will need longer, to crisp up the lower tray (or swap the trays around half way through).

Leave until completely cold, then break up into large pieces: I do this by tipping the mixture into a large bowl and breaking it up with a knife. Stir in the dried fruit and store in an airtight container. It will keep for about 2 weeks.

# Mealie meal muffins

I discovered mealie meal, a fine, pale cornmeal, during a stay in
Zimbabwe. There it is used to make the daily *sadza* (porridge) and in
breads, cakes and biscuits. These muffins can also be made using
polenta if you do not have an African or West Indian food shop nearby.
The only noticeable difference is the colour: mealie meal produces a
slightly paler muffin; polenta a lovely bright yellow one.

Whisk together the eggs, oil and milk. Sift the flour, mealie meal or polenta,
salt and baking powder into a bowl and stir in the sugar. Make a well in the
centre, then add the whisked mixture, a little at a time. Stir gently but
thoroughly to combine.

Spoon into 8 American-style muffin cases. Bake in an oven preheated to
200°C/400°F/Gas Mark 6 for about 20 minutes or until well-risen and golden
brown. Serve warm, with butter and jam.

Muffins keep better if they are made with oil rather than butter. So, if they
are destined for the cake tin rather than for immediate devouring, opt for a
recipe using oil.

## MAKES 8

| |
|---|
| 2 eggs |
| 75ml/3fl oz sunflower oil |
| 175ml/6fl oz milk |
| 110g/4oz plain flour |
| 110g/4oz mealie meal or fine polenta |
| a pinch of salt |
| 1 tablespoon baking powder |
| 50g/1¾oz caster sugar |

# Cranberry cinnamon muffins

**Substitute dried cranberries when fresh are not available.**

Whisk together the egg, oil and milk. Sift the flour and cinnamon into a bowl
and stir in the sugar. Make a well in the centre and slowly pour in the whisked
mixture. Stir until combined but do not overmix. Stir in the cranberries, mixing
well but gently. Spoon the mixture into 12 small muffin/bun paper cases (in a
bun tin) and sprinkle the tops with the demerara sugar.

Bake in an oven preheated to 180°C/350°F/Gas Mark 4 for 20–25
minutes, until golden brown on top. Serve warm.

During November and December, when the shops are full of fresh
cranberries, buy plenty and freeze so you can use them throughout the year.

## MAKES 12 SMALL MUFFINS

| |
|---|
| 1 medium egg, beaten |
| 3 tablespoons sunflower oil |
| 3 tablespoons milk |
| 140g/5oz self-raising flour |
| 1 heaped teaspoon ground cinnamon |
| 65g/2½oz caster sugar |
| 110g/4oz cranberries |
| 1 tablespoon demerara sugar |

**Cranberry cinnamon muffins**

# Banana pancakes with maple syrup

**MAKES 6**

110g/4oz self-raising flour

a pinch of salt

1 medium egg

200ml/7fl oz milk

1 teaspoon sunflower oil

2 bananas

pure maple syrup, to serve

**These thick American pancakes (called hot cakes in some States) are often served in a stack and topped with a flood of maple syrup. Savoury versions are simply dressed with butter and served with bacon, sausage and egg.**

**Use only pure maple syrup in this recipe: 'maple-flavoured' syrup might be cheap but it can also be very nasty.**

Sift the flour and salt into a bowl and make a well in the middle. Add the egg and slowly pour in the milk, whisking constantly. Add the oil and whisk until completely smooth. Cover the batter and leave to rest in the refrigerator for at least 1 hour or overnight.

Cut the bananas into thick slices on the diagonal. Rub a butter-smeared piece of paper towel all over the base of a heavy frying pan. Heat the pan, then pour in about 1½ tablespoons of the batter and top it with 3–4 banana slices. Once the pancake begins to firm up and you see tiny bubbles on the surface, flip it over, using a spatula. Cook on the other side for another minute or so – the cooking time should be about 3 minutes altogether. Keep warm (loosely covered with foil in a low oven) while you make the remaining 5 pancakes. To serve, drizzle some cold or warmed maple syrup over each pancake.

# Peanut butter and jelly muffins

**MAKES 8**

2 medium eggs

75ml/3fl oz sunflower oil

150ml/5fl oz milk

225g/8oz self-raising flour

a pinch of salt

65g/2½oz caster sugar

8 heaped teaspoons peanut butter

8 heaped teaspoons jelly

**These are a variation on that American classic, the peanut butter and jelly sandwich. Use whichever type of jelly you like – grape is typical but I prefer apple, redcurrant or quince. Serve these warm for breakfast, to peanut butter lovers like myself.**

Whisk together the eggs, oil and milk. Sift the flour and salt into a bowl and stir in the sugar. Make a well in the centre and slowly pour in the whisked liquid. Combine everything gently but thoroughly. Do not beat. Spoon half the mixture into 8 American-style muffin cases. Put a heaped teaspoonful of peanut butter on top, then one of jelly. Top with the remaining mixture, taking care to try and cover the blobs.

Bake in an oven preheated to 200°C/400°F/Gas Mark 6 for about 25 minutes or until golden brown. Serve warm.

# Lemon curd

This is an easy lemon curd recipe as it is all done in the microwave. Instead of standing stirring over a double boiler for ages, you simply put the mixture into a microwave for about half the time. It is, however, important to whisk often, otherwise you will have lemon-flavoured scrambled eggs, not fresh lemon curd.

Beat the eggs together and then strain them through a sieve. Place the butter, sugar, lemon juice and zest in a large microwave-proof bowl and cook, uncovered, on High for 3–5 minutes, until the butter has completely melted and the sugar has dissolved; stir every minute.

Cool for a couple of minutes and then gradually whisk in the eggs. Cook, uncovered, on High for about 5–8 minutes, checking and whisking every minute. Remove once the curd has thickened: you are looking for the consistency of lightly whipped cream – it will firm up on cooling. Pour into warm sterilized jars, tap the base of the jars to level the surface and cover only when completely cold. Keep the jars in the refrigerator for up to 6 weeks.

**MAKES 1.3kg/3lb**

| |
|---|
| 6 medium eggs |
| 250g/9oz unsalted butter |
| 450g/1lb granulated sugar |
| 350ml/12fl oz freshly squeezed lemon juice |
| grated zest of 6 large lemons |

# Raspberry jam with Drambuie

I think raspberry jam is the easiest of all to make, as the berries have a high pectin level and therefore should cause absolutely no problem in setting. The flavour of Drambuie goes perfectly with all sorts of summer berries, but especially with raspberries.

Place the raspberries in a preserving pan or a large saucepan (the wider the pan rim the better for jam and chutney making). Simmer very gently in their own juices until soft – about 20 minutes. Add the sugar and, stirring well, heat gently until it dissolves. Add the butter (this eliminates any scum), bring to the boil and boil rapidly for 25–30 minutes or until setting point is reached: to test, place a little jam on a cold saucer, let it cool quickly and then draw your finger through it – if it wrinkles, it is ready. Remove the pan from the heat, stir in the Drambuie and pot at once in warm sterilized jars. Either seal immediately or when completely cold. Label and store in a cool, dark place.

**MAKES 1.3kg/3lb**

| |
|---|
| 1kg/2¼lb fresh raspberries |
| 1kg/2¼lb preserving sugar |
| 15g/½oz unsalted butter |
| 1 tablespoon Drambuie |

> To sterilize jam jars, wash them well in hot soapy water and then dry in a low oven. Alternatively, if you have a dishwasher you can put them through it and then microwave on High for 1½ minutes.

**O**nce upon a time we all ate three good meals a day. Then along came fast food and the pace of our lives speeded up so much that many of us now eat on the hoof or graze as the day goes on. However unhealthy or disagreeable this might seem to traditionalists, it is a part of our hectic lives and so we might as well accept the fact. Besides, provided we have a nourishing snack instead of a bag of crisps or bar of chocolate, why not? It means there is more time to save the planet, compose a symphony or just flop on the sofa with a good book.

Most of the recipes in this chapter are quick to produce and are suitable either for a light supper or lunch or for a snack at any time of day. Try the Three-tomato tart on page 81 for a casual summer lunch with friends, the Hot pork and apple loaf on page 79 for the children's tea or Poached eggs on pesto toast, page 71, for a midnight snack. Those who suffer middle-of-the-night hunger pangs, which are often appeased by a quick bowl of cereal or a pile of buttered toast, will hopefully be tempted by some of the dishes here, too.

CHAPTER FIVE
# snacks and lunches

# Prawns with coconut

**SERVES 4**

2 tablespoons olive oil

1 garlic clove, crushed

1 onion, finely chopped

3 tablespoons chopped fresh parsley, plus extra to garnish

5 tablespoons creamed tomatoes (from a carton)

125g/4½oz creamed coconut, grated (it is easier to do this in a food processor)

500g/1lb 2oz peeled cooked prawns, thawed and well drained if frozen

a pinch of cayenne pepper

salt and freshly ground black pepper

**This is based on a recipe from Brazilian friends. The dish they cook in Rio is much hotter, with extra chilli added. It is also a richer colour, for the cooking fat they use is crimson-coloured *dende* oil (palm oil from the *dende* palm tree). Serve with some buttered rice and a tomato salad.**

Heat the oil in a saucepan, add the garlic and onion and fry gently for 5 minutes. Stir in the parsley and creamed tomatoes and cook for a further 5 minutes. Add the coconut and stir carefully to melt it down. Then add the prawns and 2 tablespoons of water and cook gently for about 10 minutes. Season to taste with the cayenne pepper and some salt and pepper. Serve hot, with a sprinkling of parsley.

## A tropical lunch

**Tom yam soup**     31

**Prawns with coconut**

**Banana and lime ice-cream with chocolate sauce**     163

## Joanna's wine notes

A tangy, fruity, New World Sauvignon Blanc, especially from New Zealand, goes well with the prawns with coconut and, for those who want wine with their soup, will also handle the assertive flavours of chilli, coriander and lemongrass.

# Baked truffled eggs

**Be sure to use a truffle oil based on extra virgin olive oil; cheaper versions are made with inferior oils that give very little flavour. Truffle oil makes a good flavouring for risotto, pasta or potato gratins. But use only a tiny amount – count on no more than 1 teaspoon per person.**

Whisk together the crème fraîche and Parmesan cheese, then season generously with salt and pepper. Butter 8 medium (7.5cm/3in) ramekins and divide the mixture between them. Break an egg into each and top with 1 teaspoon of the oil. Pour carefully: overdo the oil at this stage and you will ruin the dish.

Place on a baking tray and bake in an oven preheated to 200°C/400°F/Gas Mark 6 for 10–14 minutes, until the egg whites are just set but the yolks still runny. Serve with plenty of Granary toast to dunk.

## SERVES 8

| |
|---|
| 400ml/14fl oz crème fraîche |
| 75g/2¾oz Parmesan cheese, freshly grated |
| 8 medium free-range eggs |
| 8 teaspoons truffle oil |
| salt and freshly ground black pepper |

# Sauna sausage with new potato salad

**Many Finns cook *makkara*, their much-loved smoked sausage, over the sauna stones after (and during) a sauna. The sauna ritual involves splashing bucketloads of water on to the stones to increase the heat from far-too-hot to unbearable. If it is a sauna party (women first, men later – don't panic) some beer might be taken in. Besides being drunk, it is also splashed on to the sauna stones to give off the fabulous yeasty aroma of freshly baked bread. After the beer come the sausages: these are either placed directly on the stones or wrapped in foil first. If you don't happen to have a sauna to hand, cook the sausage under the grill or on a barbecue.**

Boil the potatoes in salted water until tender, then drain well. Mix together the mayonnaise, soured cream, mustard, herbs and vinegar and season with salt and pepper to taste. Pour this dressing over the hot potatoes, stirring gently to coat them. Leave to cool, then add the apple, gherkin and spring onions.

Grill or barbecue the sausage and then serve it with the potato salad and plenty of mustard.

## SERVES 4

| |
|---|
| 750g/1lb 10oz new potatoes, scrubbed |
| 2 tablespoons mayonnaise |
| 150ml/5fl oz soured cream |
| ½ teaspoon English mustard |
| 1 tablespoon chopped fresh tarragon or chervil |
| 1 teaspoon white wine vinegar |
| 1 crisp apple, cored and diced |
| 1 large gherkin, chopped |
| 3 spring onions, chopped |
| 1 smoked sausage ring |
| salt and freshly ground black pepper |

# Anchovy and spinach tart

## SERVES 6

100g jar of anchovies in olive oil

2 garlic cloves, chopped

6 spring onions, chopped

175g/6oz fresh spinach, shredded

200ml/7fl oz crème fraîche

3 medium eggs

freshly ground black pepper

### For the pastry:

175g/6oz plain flour, sifted

50g/1¾oz fine polenta

½ teaspoon salt

125g/4½oz unsalted butter, cubed

1 medium egg

1 tablespoon olive oil

**If you use salted anchovies instead of ones preserved in oil, be sure to rinse them really well.**

For the pastry, put the flour, polenta, salt and butter in a food processor and process briefly until the mixture resembles breadcrumbs. Whisk together the egg and olive oil and add through the feeder tube with the machine running. After a few seconds, gather the pastry into a ball, wrap in clingfilm and refrigerate for 1 hour. Roll it out thinly to fit a 28cm/11in loose-bottomed tart tin. Prick the base, then refrigerate for at least 2 hours or overnight. Line the pastry case with foil and fill with baking beans. Bake blind for 15 minutes at 190°C/375°F/Gas Mark 5, then remove the foil and beans and bake for a further 5 minutes.

Meanwhile, prepare the filling. Heat 2 tablespoons of oil from the jar of anchovies in a frying pan, add the garlic and spring onions and fry gently for 3 minutes. Stir in the spinach and cook until wilted (1–2 minutes), then remove from the heat. Beat the crème fraîche with the eggs and plenty of pepper (no salt), then add the spinach mixture, stirring well. Carefully ladle this into the tart. Drain the anchovies and arrange them like wheel spokes on top of the flan. Bake for 30–35 minutes, until golden brown. Serve warm.

# Tomato and Marmite bruschetta

## SERVES 4

4 plum tomatoes, skinned and chopped

5–6 basil leaves, chopped

1 tablespoon olive oil

4 thick slices of sourdough/country bread

1 large garlic clove, halved

Marmite

salt and freshly ground black pepper

**Err on the side of caution with the Marmite, and choose tomatoes with bags of intense, ripe flavour.**

Mix together the tomatoes, basil and oil with some salt and pepper to taste. Toast or grill the bread, then rub the cut garlic clove all over one side. Spread each piece of toast thinly with Marmite, then pile on the tomatoes and their juices. Serve at once.

> When making bruschetta, after rubbing a cut clove of garlic over the toast, rub in a cut half of tomato for added flavour and colour.

# Poached eggs on pesto toast

**It is important to use really fresh eggs for poaching.**

To poach the eggs, heat a wide, shallow pan of water until it is simmering gently, then break an egg into a cup and slide it into the water: cook 3 eggs at a time. Using a slotted spoon, carefully draw the whites in around the yolks and cook until done to your liking (about 2–3 minutes). Meanwhile, make the toast, then spread it generously with pesto.

Carefully remove the eggs from the pan with a slotted spoon and drain on kitchen paper. Season with salt and pepper and place one egg on each pesto toast. Serve at once, with tomato slices and Parmesan shavings if you like.

**SERVES 6**

6 large free-range eggs

6 large, thick slices of bread (I use sourdough)

pesto sauce

salt and freshly ground black pepper

tomato slices and Parmesan shavings, to serve (optional)

# Walnut bread with goat's cheese

**If you are serving this bread on the day you bake it, just slice it and serve with spreadable goat's cheese. Any later, then toast thick slices and top with chilled cheese.**

Place the flours in a bowl and stir in the dried yeast and salt. Make a well in the centre, add the oil and water and mix everything together with a spoon to make a soft but not sticky dough. Gather it up with your hands and place on a lightly floured board. With floured hands, knead for about 10 minutes or until the dough feels smooth and elastic. (To knead, stretch the dough away with the heel of your hand, fold it back, give it a quarter turn, then repeat.) Place the dough in a lightly oiled bowl and cover. Leave somewhere barely warm for 1½–2 hours or until well risen. When you insert a finger into the dough it should not spring back.

Turn the dough out on to a board and punch down to knock out the air, then knead in the walnuts. Butter a 1kg/2¼lb loaf tin. Shape the dough into a rectangle the length of the tin. Roll up, then tuck in the ends underneath. Place the loaf, seam-side down, in the tin and cover lightly with oiled clingfilm. Leave somewhere barely warm for about 30 minutes, until it has risen to fill the tin. Bake in an oven preheated to 230°C/450°F/Gas Mark 8 for 20 minutes, then reduce the heat to 200°C/400°F/Gas Mark 6 and bake for a further 20–25 minutes or until the loaf sounds hollow when tapped on the base. Leave to cool on a wire rack before slicing and spreading with the goat's cheese.

**MAKES 1 LOAF**

400g/14oz strong white flour

100g/3½oz Granary flour

6g sachet of easy-blend dried yeast

1 teaspoon salt

2 tablespoons walnut or olive oil

300ml/10fl oz tepid (hand-hot) water

75g/2¾oz walnuts, chopped

soft goat's cheese, to serve

# Oregano cornbread

**SERVES 6–8**

250g/9oz plain flour

1 level tablespoon baking powder

150g/5½oz cornmeal or polenta

1 teaspoon salt

2 tablespoons chopped fresh oregano

250ml/9fl oz milk

75g/2¾oz butter, melted

2 medium eggs

40g/1½oz caster sugar

**Although American cornmeal (not cornflour) is rather more finely ground than Italian polenta, the latter is perfectly good for this recipe. In the States you will find cornmeal in biscuits (similar to our scones), spoonbread (a soufflé-like dish) and grits (like porridge). This cornbread is divine eaten on its own or served with fiery chilli con carne, hearty soups or stews.**

Sift the flour and baking powder into a bowl and stir in the cornmeal, salt and oregano. Mix the milk with the melted butter and stir it into the flour mixture. Beat the eggs with the sugar and add. Stir everything together gently but thoroughly, then pour into a buttered 23cm/9in square tin. Bake in an oven preheated to 220°C/425°F/Gas Mark 7 for about 30 minutes, until well risen and golden brown. Leave in the tin for 5–10 minutes, then turn out on to a wire rack to cool. Cut into squares to serve.

# Potato and herb bread

**MAKES 4 LARGE ROLLS**

225g/8oz potatoes (peeled weight)

25g/1oz unsalted butter

400g/14oz strong white flour, sifted

3 tablespoons chopped fresh herbs

6g sachet of easy-blend dried yeast

15g/½oz caster sugar

1 level tablespoon salt

200–225ml/7–8fl oz warm milk

**Chives, parsley and tarragon are all good in these light, moist rolls. Golden Wonder, King Edward and Maris Piper are suitable varieties of potato. Serve with soup or salad for lunch.**

Boil the potatoes in unsalted water until tender, then drain thoroughly. Mash with the butter until smooth. Stir the flour, herbs, yeast, sugar and salt together in a mixing bowl. While the potatoes are still warm, stir them into the flour mixture with just enough warm milk to make a fairly soft but not sticky dough. Using well-floured hands, turn the mixture out on to a floured board and knead for about 5 minutes or until fairly smooth. Place in a clean bowl and cover with clingfilm. Leave to rise somewhere warm for about 1 hour, until almost doubled in size.

Knock back the risen dough. Using floured hands, divide the mixture into 4 and shape each into a round. Place on a lightly buttered baking sheet, sprinkle lightly with flour and leave to rise again for about 30 minutes or until puffed up. Bake in an oven preheated to 220°C/425°F/Gas Mark 7 for about 20 minutes or until golden brown. Transfer to a wire rack to cool. Serve warm with butter.

# Thai fish balls with dipping sauce

**This is my variation on a recipe by the South Australian chef Maggie Beer. Serve as a starter or as canapés.**

For the fish balls, place the fish in a food processor and, using the pulse button, process briefly until chopped. Don't overdo it or you may end up with a paste. Add all the remaining ingredients except the sunflower oil and process for a few seconds to combine. Shape into 12 balls, using dampened hands. Chill for at least 1 hour.

For the dipping sauce, put the sugar, vinegar, fish sauce, soy sauce and lime juice in a saucepan and bring slowly to the boil. Remove from the heat, pour into a bowl and leave to cool, then stir in the chilli and coriander.

Heat the sunflower oil in a frying pan until hot, then add the fish balls. Fry for about 5 minutes, turning, until golden brown and crisp. Serve hot, with the dipping sauce.

## SERVES 6

300g/10½oz cod or haddock fillet, roughly chopped

1 tablespoon freshly grated root ginger

3 spring onions, finely chopped

4 fresh basil leaves, chopped

1 tablespoon chopped fresh coriander

1 garlic clove, chopped

a dash of hot chilli sauce

1 teaspoon dark soy sauce

1½ tablespoons coconut milk (from a tin)

2 teaspoons Thai fish sauce (*nam pla*)

2 tablespoons sunflower oil

**For the dipping sauce:**

2 level tablespoons molasses sugar

5 tablespoons white wine vinegar

1 tablespoon Thai fish sauce (*nam pla*)

1 tablespoon dark soy sauce

juice of 1 lime

½ red chilli, deseeded and finely chopped

1 tablespoon chopped fresh coriander

# Aubergine and feta sandwich

## SERVES 6

250g/9oz feta cheese

2 plum tomatoes, skinned and finely diced

¼ cucumber, finely diced

¼ red chilli, chopped

2 heaped tablespoons chopped fresh dill

2 large aubergines

olive oil for frying

freshly ground black pepper

**This Turkish-inspired dish is one of contrasting temperatures and textures: a cold, creamy feta filling sandwiched between two warm slices of grilled aubergine.**

Mash the feta cheese in a bowl until soft, or cut it into cubes, then stir in the tomatoes, cucumber, chilli, dill and plenty of black pepper.

Cut each aubergine lengthways into 6 slices. Heat some olive oil in a large frying pan and fry the aubergine slices in batches until tender and golden brown on both sides. Place one aubergine slice on each serving plate. Spread over the feta mixture and top with another aubergine slice. Leave for a couple of minutes for the heat of the aubergine to melt the feta mixture slightly, then serve.

# Chicken livers with toasted brioche and gherkins

## SERVES 4

20g/¾oz butter

2 tablespoons olive oil

4 large garlic cloves, chopped

1 onion, finely chopped

600g/1lb 5oz chicken livers, trimmed

4 large (or 8 small) slices of brioche

a large jar of pickled gherkins, drained and sliced lengthways

2 tablespoons Marsala (or medium sherry)

1 tablespoon chopped fresh flat-leaf parsley

salt and freshly ground black pepper

**Use either one large brioche or four individual ones, cut into thick slices.**

Heat the butter and oil in a frying pan, add the garlic and onion and fry gently for about 10 minutes, until softened. Increase the heat and add the chicken livers (they will splutter; prepare to wash the cooker). Fry over a high heat for about 4–5 minutes, turning once, until they are nicely browned but still soft and pink inside. Meanwhile, toast the brioche and place the gherkins in a serving dish.

Season the chicken livers generously with salt and pepper, then switch off the heat. Pour in the Marsala and stir well.

Put the toasted brioche slices on 4 warm serving plates and place the chicken livers on top, then slowly pour over the sauce, ensuring that each slice of brioche is lightly moistened. Sprinkle over the parsley and serve at once with the gherkins.

# Baked tomato eggs

**SERVES 4**

4 large tomatoes

4 medium free-range eggs

salt and freshly ground black pepper

**These baked eggs sit snugly in hollowed-out tomatoes, not only looking good but also tasting delicious. All they need is a mountain of toast for dipping purposes.**

Slice the top off each tomato and scoop out the insides and seeds with a spoon. Turn upside down on a piece of kitchen paper to drain away any liquid. It is important to keep changing the paper until it seems completely dry, otherwise the eggs will become watery when baked.

Place the tomatoes in a lightly oiled baking dish and crack an egg into each one. Season generously with salt and pepper, then place in an oven preheated to 180°C/350°F/Gas Mark 4. Bake for 20–25 minutes or until the eggs are just set. Serve at once, with a pile of hot buttered toast.

# Calzone with Taleggio, garlic and spinach

**SERVES 2**

225g/8oz strong white flour

1 teaspoon salt

6g sachet of easy-blend dried yeast

2 tablespoons olive oil, plus extra for brushing

125–150ml/4–5fl oz tepid (hand-hot) water

200g/7oz fresh spinach

3 garlic cloves, chopped

110g/4oz Taleggio cheese, cut into slices

salt and freshly ground black pepper

**This Cornish pasty of the pizza world is deeply satisfying. It not only looks inviting once cut into, revealing the dark green spinach spilling over the gooey, melting cheese, it also tastes wonderful. If you cannot find Taleggio (a soft cow's milk cheese from Lombardy), use Reblochon instead.**

Sift the flour and salt into a bowl and stir in the yeast. Make a well in the middle and pour in 1 tablespoon of the oil and enough water to form a stiff dough. Now get in with your hands and gather the dough together into a ball. Turn out on to a lightly floured board and knead for about 10 minutes or until smooth and elastic. Place in a lightly oiled bowl, cover and leave somewhere barely warm for about 1 hour or until almost doubled in size.

Meanwhile, prepare the filling: wash the spinach thoroughly and place in a large saucepan with only the water clinging to its leaves. Cook for a couple of minutes until it wilts, then remove and drain well over a sieve, squeezing out all the water. Heat the remaining oil in a pan and fry the garlic for 2 minutes, then add the spinach and cook for 2–3 minutes. Set aside to cool.

Turn the dough out on to a board and punch down. Then stretch it into a circle about 25–28cm/10–11in in diameter. Place the slices of cheese over one half of the circle, leaving a rim. Place the spinach on top, then season well. Fold over the other half of the dough and press the edges firmly together. Brush with olive oil and leave somewhere warm for 15–20 minutes.

Bake in an oven preheated to 230°C/450°F/Gas Mark 8 for 20 minutes, then remove and brush with olive oil. Serve at once.

# Asparagus with soft-boiled eggs

Although we are now fortunate enough to have imported asparagus throughout the year, it is still very exciting when the first local asparagus comes into the shops. Call me partisan, but to my taste nothing quite beats the flavour of British asparagus. And although the French and Germans rate white asparagus as the best I find it both tasteless and uninteresting, deprived as it is of the merest suggestion of sunshine by being cut below ground.

This dish is simplicity itself ... but what raptures of delight it provokes. Do not choose thin asparagus spears; the sturdier they are, the better.

Snap off any woody ends from the asparagus and wash the spears. Cook them in boiling water for 5–8 minutes or until just tender. Drain well, then pile on a plate, preferably wrapped in a napkin.

While the asparagus is cooking, boil the eggs: place them in a pan of cold water and bring slowly to the boil, then boil for 3 minutes. Drain the eggs and put in egg cups.

To serve, put an egg cup on each serving plate and cut off the top of the eggs. Season with salt and pepper, then dip the asparagus into the eggs and eat with buttered toast.

## SERVES 2

300–350g/10½–12oz asparagus spears

2 large free-range eggs

salt and freshly ground black pepper

a mountain of buttered toast, to serve

# Courgettes with garlic and cream

This can be served as a light meal with crusty bread or as an accompaniment to grilled meat. You can also add a grating of lemon zest to the cream.

Trim the ends of the courgettes and cut them lengthways into slices – about 5 per courgette. Heat the butter in a large frying pan and fry the courgettes (in batches) for about 5 minutes, turning once, until beginning to colour. Using a slotted spoon, transfer to an ovenproof dish and season well.

Put the cream and garlic in a saucepan and heat until bubbles appear on the surface, then pour this mixture over the courgettes. Sprinkle over the Parmesan. Bake in an oven preheated to 190°C/375°F/Gas Mark 5 for 20–25 minutes, until golden brown.

## SERVES 4

600g/1lb 5oz courgettes

25g/1oz butter

150ml/5fl oz double cream

2 large garlic cloves, chopped

1 heaped tablespoon freshly grated Parmesan cheese

salt and freshly ground black pepper

# Hot pork and apple loaf

**Use a wide, fairly long loaf of bread, weighing about 450g/1lb.**

Cut the loaf in half horizontally, keeping the two sides hinged together. With your fingers, remove as much of the soft crumb as possible.

Heat 1 teaspoon of the oil in a pan and fry the onion for about 3 minutes, until softened, then add the pork and brown all over. Add the paprika, tomato purée and some salt and pepper and cook, uncovered, for 25 minutes, stirring occasionally. Then leave to cool for at least 20 minutes.

Beat the cream cheese with a spoon to soften it and then spread it inside both halves of the loaf. Spoon the meat into one half, packing it down well. Spread the grated apples over the top of this and sprinkle the Cheddar over the apple. Drizzle the remaining oil over the top, then close the loaf, pressing down carefully. Wrap tightly in a double layer of lightly oiled foil and bake in an oven preheated to 200°C/400°F/Gas Mark 6 for 20–30 minutes or until the cheese has melted and everything is hot. Wait for 10 minutes, then using a sharp (preferably electric) knife, cut into thick slices and serve.

**SERVES 8**

| |
|---|
| 1 thick French loaf |
| 3 teaspoons olive oil |
| 1 small onion, finely chopped |
| 400g/14oz lean minced pork |
| 1 teaspoon paprika |
| 1 tablespoon tomato purée |
| 200g/7oz cream cheese with garlic and herbs |
| 2 medium (or 1 large) Granny Smith apples, peeled and grated |
| 110g/4oz Cheddar cheese, grated |
| salt and freshly ground black pepper |

# Prawn, avocado and cheese quesadillas

**These Mexican-inspired turnovers are delicious served straight from the oven with a dollop of salsa – I like cactus salsa but if you cannot find that, use a chilli-zapped tomato one instead. Serve 2 or 3 per person, depending on appetite. I could eat 4 easily but this seems a little on the greedy side, especially if I'm making them for guests – unless it is guests who are already aware of my rampant gluttony.**

Place the tortillas on a large board and cut them in half. Carefully smear ½ teaspoon of mustard over each half, spreading it right out to the edges (this helps seal them).

Mix together the prawns, mayonnaise and chives and season with salt and pepper. Divide this mixture between the tortilla halves, placing a little mound on one side of each semi-circle. Top with 2 slices of avocado (you might need to halve them), then squeeze over a little lemon juice. Sprinkle over the grated cheese and close up each tortilla. Seal the edges by pressing them firmly together (but don't worry if bits poke out).

Put the quesadillas on an oiled baking tray and bake in an oven preheated to 200°C/400°F/Gas Mark 6 for 8–10 minutes, until golden brown. Serve at once, with a dollop of cactus or tomato salsa.

**MAKES 8**

| |
|---|
| 4 large, soft flour tortillas |
| 4 teaspoons Dijon mustard |
| 200g/7oz cooked shelled prawns, thawed and well-drained if frozen |
| 1 heaped tablespoon mayonnaise |
| 1 tablespoon chopped fresh chives |
| 1 large avocado, peeled, stoned and cut into 16 slices |
| lemon juice |
| 100g/3½oz mature Cheddar cheese, grated |
| salt and freshly ground black pepper |

# Mushroom risotto cakes

**MAKES 4**

about 2½ tablespoons olive oil

½ onion, finely chopped

150g/5½oz mushrooms, chopped

200g/7oz arborio rice

750ml/1¼ pints hot chicken stock

25g/1oz Parmesan cheese, freshly grated

1 heaped tablespoon chopped fresh oregano

1 egg, beaten

salt and freshly ground black pepper

**These versatile risotto cakes can be served with fresh tomato sauce or pesto and a grating of Parmesan. Or you can use them to accompany grilled meats, as an interesting alternative to a rice or potato dish. I also like them served just as they are – soft and squishy inside, crusty outside – with perhaps a soft poached egg on top if I am feeling self-indulgent.**

Heat 1½ tablespoons of the oil in a heavy-based pan, add the onion and mushrooms and fry gently for about 10 minutes, until softened. Add the rice and stir well to coat with the oil. Gradually add the hot stock, ladle by ladle, stirring until it is absorbed before adding the next batch: it should take about 20 minutes altogether for all the stock to be incorporated and the rice to be tender. Then season well with salt and pepper, stir in the cheese and oregano and leave for about 10 minutes. Stir in the beaten egg, then pour the mixture into a clingfilm-lined 23cm/9in square baking tin. Leave until cold and then refrigerate for at least 1 hour.

Lift the chilled risotto mixture out of the tin and peel off the clingfilm. Cut into 4 squares. Heat about 1 tablespoon of olive oil in a large frying pan and add 2 of the risotto cakes. Fry for about 5 minutes on each side until golden brown and crusty. Continue with the other 2 cakes (adding a little more oil if necessary). Serve warm.

# Leeks with mustard and cheese

**SERVES 4 AS AN ACCOMPANIMENT**

600g/1lb 5oz young leeks

50g/1¾oz unsalted butter, softened

2 tablespoons coarsegrain mustard

50g/1¾oz Cheddar cheese, grated

salt and freshly ground black pepper

**This dish can be served either as a vegetarian main course or as an accompaniment to roast or grilled meat. Use a well-flavoured mature cheese such as farmhouse Cheddar.**

If the leeks are small, keep them whole. Otherwise, cut them diagonally into thick slices. Steam them for 5–8 minutes, depending on size. Test with a knife to check if they are cooked; they should still be slightly crisp.

Meanwhile, beat together the softened butter, mustard, cheese and some salt and pepper.

Drain the cooked leeks really well and place them in a heatproof shallow dish. Dot with the mustard butter and place under a preheated grill for 3–5 minutes, until bubbly and golden brown. Serve immediately.

# Three-tomato tart

This tart has light, buttery pastry and a creamy filling flavoured with 3 different types of tomato. The drizzle of basil and oil at the end makes it look – and taste – even nicer. Serve with a green salad.

For the pastry, put the flour, salt and butter in a food processor and process briefly. Mix together the egg yolk and oil and pour through the feeder tube. Process briefly until the mixture is moist but not wet or sticky (you might need to add a drop or two of water). Combine with your hands, wrap in clingfilm and chill for about 1 hour. Then roll out to fit a 23cm/9in loose-bottomed tart tin. Prick the base all over with a fork and chill for at least 2 hours, preferably overnight. Line with foil and fill with baking beans, then bake blind in an oven preheated to 200°C/400°F/Gas Mark 6 for 15 minutes. Remove the foil and beans and bake for 5 minutes longer. Leave to cool. Reduce the oven temperature to 190°C/375°F/Gas Mark 5.

For the filling, whisk the mascarpone, Cheddar and eggs together with plenty of salt and pepper. Cut the plum tomatoes into quarters and the cherry tomatoes in half and place them upside down on kitchen paper to drain. Once they are dry, arrange them cut-side up in the tart, interspersing them with the sun-dried tomatoes. Season with salt and pepper and pour over the mascarpone mixture.

Whizz together the basil leaves and oil in a blender (don't worry if it doesn't become a smooth purée; it should just be a rough mixture), then drizzle this slowly over the tart. Bake for about 35 minutes, until puffed up and golden brown. Leave for at least 20 minutes before serving warm.

## SERVES 4

250g/9oz mascarpone cheese

50g/1¾oz mature Cheddar cheese, grated

2 large eggs

2 plum tomatoes

9 cherry tomatoes

6 sun-dried tomatoes, halved

1 tablespoon fresh basil leaves

2 tablespoons extra virgin olive oil

salt and freshly ground black pepper

**For the pastry:**

250g/9oz plain flour, sifted

¼ teaspoon salt

100g/3½oz unsalted butter, diced

1 medium egg yolk

1½–2 tablespoons oil (from the jar of sun-dried tomatoes)

We've all been there – late home from work, exhausted, frazzled and hungry, in need of sustenance but without the strength to wait for much longer than half an hour to fill our ravenous bodies. Any longer and a severe sense of humour failure might ensue. The shopping has probably been done in a rush on the way home, so this is not the time to tackle recipes calling for buckwheat polenta, Aboriginal wattle seeds or Japanese wasabi. What is required is a good, sensible recipe that is relatively quick to rustle up and strong on flavour.

Think about it: if you are absolutely ravenous do you really want a delicately flavoured little fillet of sole or bland-tasting chunk of steamed tofu? No, you want gutsy flavours that pack a punch and leave you in absolutely no doubt that your hungry yearnings have been satisfied and you are now filled with an invigorating sense of energy. Then again, you might be so content after such a delicious supper that you feel the onset of a deep lethargy and the lure of the armchair becomes far too appealing.

# CHAPTER SIX
# after-work suppers

# Chicken breasts with spinach, tomato and mozzarella

## SERVES 4

25g/1oz butter

4 boneless free-range chicken breasts, skinned

250g/9oz fresh spinach

freshly grated nutmeg

75g/2¾oz mozzarella cheese, grated

salt and freshly ground black pepper

**For the tomato sauce:**

1 tablespoon olive oil

1 onion, chopped

2 garlic cloves, chopped

400g tin of chopped tomatoes

5–6 fresh basil leaves

**This dish is simple, tasty and very colourful. All it requires is a side salad, sauté potatoes and crusty white bread ... oh, and four very hungry people.**

For the sauce, heat the oil in a saucepan and gently fry the onion and garlic until softened – about 10 minutes. Stir in the tomatoes, basil and some salt and pepper, then cook, covered, for about 20 minutes, until thickened. Purée in a food processor or blender and check the seasoning.

Heat the butter in a frying pan and quickly brown the chicken all over. Season with salt and pepper. Meanwhile, lightly cook the spinach by steaming or microwaving it for 2–3 minutes. Drain well, then season with salt, pepper and a tiny grating of nutmeg.

To assemble, place the spinach in an ovenproof dish, then put the chicken on top. Pour over the tomato sauce and sprinkle over the grated mozzarella. Cook in an oven preheated to 190°C/375°F/Gas Mark 5 for about 25 minutes or until the chicken is cooked through and the mozzarella has melted. Serve piping hot.

# Barley risotto

## SERVES 6-8

40g/1½oz dried porcini mushrooms

750ml/1¼ pints hot chicken (or vegetable) stock

75g/2¾oz unsalted butter

3 garlic cloves, chopped

1 large onion, chopped

500g/1lb 2oz pearl barley

1 tablespoon Worcestershire sauce

1 teaspoon salt

2 tablespoons chopped fresh flat-leaf parsley

freshly ground black pepper

freshly grated Parmesan cheese, to serve (optional)

**You can substitute 300g/10½oz fresh mushrooms for the dried: slice them and add with the garlic and onion at the beginning.**

Rinse the dried mushrooms and then soak them in the hot stock for about 30 minutes. Melt the butter in a large flameproof casserole, add the garlic and onion and fry gently for about 10 minutes, until softened. Add the barley, stir well to coat with the butter, then add the Worcestershire sauce, soaked mushrooms and stock. Bring to the boil, stirring, then add the salt and plenty of black pepper. Cover tightly, remove from the heat and place in an oven preheated to 170°C/325°F/Gas Mark 3 for about 30–35 minutes or until the liquid has been absorbed by the barley. Taste for seasoning and stir in the parsley. Serve immediately, with or without grated Parmesan.

# Pasta with mushrooms

Use button or chestnut mushrooms unless you are lucky enough to get your hands on some fresh wild ones during their all-too-short season. The dried wild ones, such as porcini (ceps), morels or chanterelles, are wonderful for the rest of the year.

Rinse the dried porcini well and then soak them in the wine for 30 minutes. Drain and reserve the liquid.

Heat the oil in a large saucepan and gently fry the shallots and garlic for 2–3 minutes. Add both the fresh and dried mushrooms, stirring well. Cook over a gentle heat for about 5 minutes. Increase the heat to medium, stir in the reserved mushroom-soaking liquid and cook, uncovered, for about 10 minutes or until the liquid has reduced by about half. Add the cream and continue cooking for 4–5 minutes, stirring occasionally. Remove from the heat and stir in the grated Parmesan. Add the soy sauce and plenty of pepper. Taste and add extra soy and pepper if required (you will not need much – if any – salt as the soy is salty).

Meanwhile, cook the pasta in a large pan of boiling salted water until *al dente* and then drain thoroughly. Tip the pasta into the pan of mushroom sauce and toss well, then transfer to a large warmed serving bowl. Shave some Parmesan (from a block) over the top and serve.

## SERVES 4

25g/1oz dried porcini mushrooms

350ml/12fl oz dry white wine

2 tablespoons olive oil

3 large shallots, chopped

2 large garlic cloves, chopped

400g/14oz mushrooms, chopped

150ml/5fl oz double cream

50g/1¾oz Parmesan cheese, freshly grated

2 teaspoons light soy sauce

300g/10½oz dried pappardelle or tagliatelle

salt and freshly ground black pepper

Parmesan shavings (shaved with a potato peeler), to serve

## Storecupboard supper

**Artichoke, rocket and Parmesan salad**  40

**Pasta with mushrooms**

**Caramelized apples with melted toffee**  158

### Joanna's wine notes
A young, medium-full Chardonnay (e.g. Vin de Pays d'Oc or New World) would carry you through both the salad and pasta but, if your wine rack runs to it, pick a lively young white to go with the salad (Hungarian, Sancerre, Sauvignon), then a richer white (a Chardonnay) or a velvety red, such as a Rioja, Navarra or Romanian Merlot, to match the mushrooms.

# Mussels with chilli and coriander

**If you have a high chilli tolerance, add one extra.**

Scrub and de-beard the mussels, discarding any with broken shells or any open ones that do not close when tapped on a work surface. Place the mussels in a large saucepan with the wine. Bring to the boil, then cover and cook over a high heat for 4–5 minutes, shaking the pan occasionally, until the shells have opened. Discard any mussels that have not opened, then strain the liquid through a double layer of muslin (or kitchen paper) into a bowl.

Heat the oil in a large pan and gently fry the garlic and shallots for about 2 minutes. Add the leek and chillies and fry for 3 minutes. Increase the heat, add the passata and strained mussel liquor and bring to the boil. Cook over a high heat until the mixture reduces and begins to thicken, then add the sun-dried tomatoes and most of the coriander and parsley. Lower the heat and cook for a further 2–3 minutes, then season to taste.

Add the mussels to the pan and reheat gently for 2–3 minutes. Tip into a warmed tureen, sprinkle over the reserved coriander and parsley and serve.

> If you suffer 'chilli burn' while preparing chillies, bathe the affected part of your body in milk before washing with soap and water.

**SERVES 4**

| |
|---|
| 1kg/2¼lb fresh mussels |
| 150ml/5fl oz dry white wine |
| 2 tablespoons olive oil |
| 2 garlic cloves, finely chopped |
| 4 shallots, finely chopped |
| 1 large leek, chopped |
| 2 fresh red chillies, deseeded and chopped |
| 450ml/16fl oz tomato passata |
| 2 tablespoons chopped sun-dried tomatoes |
| 3 tablespoons chopped fresh coriander |
| 2 tablespoons chopped fresh parsley |
| salt and freshly ground black pepper |

# Cod with black olive salsa

**Ask your fishmonger for thick pieces of cod, preferably middle-cut fillets, weighing about 150g/5½oz each.**
**Serve with some steamed red rice and Roast Fennel (see page 153).**

Place the cod on a small oiled baking tray and season well. Pour ½ tablespoon of wine and 1 teaspoon of olive oil over the top of each fillet. Bake in an oven preheated to 230°C/450°F/Gas Mark 8 for 8–10 minutes or until just cooked.

Meanwhile, make the salsa: put the olives, tomatoes, oil and lemon juice in a small saucepan and heat until very warm (do not boil). Remove from the heat and stir in the basil and some salt and pepper to taste. To serve, slide the cod on to warmed plates and spoon over the warm olive salsa.

**SERVES 2**

| |
|---|
| 2 thick cod fillets, skinned |
| 1 tablespoon dry white wine |
| 2 teaspoons olive oil |
| salt and freshly ground black pepper |

**For the salsa:**

| |
|---|
| 12–16 black olives, stoned and diced |
| 2 plum tomatoes, skinned and diced |
| 2 tablespoons olive oil |
| 1 tablespoon lemon juice |
| 1 tablespoon shredded fresh basil |

**Cod with black olive salsa**

# Trout with *chermoula* crust

## SERVES 4

4 large trout fillets

olive oil for brushing

salt and freshly ground black pepper

### For the crust:

100g/3½oz fresh breadcrumbs

3 tablespoons fresh mint leaves

3 tablespoons fresh coriander leaves

1½ teaspoons ground cumin

a large pinch of cayenne pepper

2 garlic cloves, chopped

juice of 1 lemon

2 tablespoons olive oil

**This Moroccan-style crust is based on *chermoula,* a dry-spice marinade for fish and poultry, flavoured with coriander, parsley, onion, garlic and cumin. I have added some breadcrumbs (I use wholemeal or rye) to form a thick crust that becomes nicely crunchy after grilling. Serve with some olive oil-dressed couscous.**

Put all the ingredients for the crust in a food processor and whizz until well combined.

Brush the fish with a little olive oil, season with salt and pepper and place, skin-side down, on a grill pan. Cook under a preheated grill for about 3 minutes, then remove. Spread the *chermoula* paste gently over the top of the fillets. Grill for a further 4–5 minutes or until the fish is cooked through: test with the tip of a sharp knife.

# Beef with black bean sauce and noodles

## SERVES 4

500g/1lb 2oz rump steak, cut into strips

2 tablespoons sunflower oil

2 heaped teaspoons freshly grated root ginger

150g/5½oz mangetout

1 red pepper, deseeded and cut into slivers

1 tablespoon dry sherry

200g jar of black bean sauce

300g/10½oz oriental noodles

a dash of sesame oil

salt and freshly ground black pepper

**Use any form of oriental noodle – egg, wheat, rice or the Japanese buckwheat noodles called soba. And remember that, alien as it is to British sensibilities, it is perfectly acceptable to eat hot noodles with a sucking noise, as they do in Asia. The noise is in fact a cooling intake of breath. Throw caution to the wind and slurp.**

Heat a wok or heavy frying pan. Meanwhile, mix the beef with 1 tablespoon of the sunflower oil and the ginger, stirring to coat. Once the pan is extremely hot, add the beef (in 2 batches – do not crowd the pan). Stir-fry for about 2 minutes, then transfer to a dish. Season with salt and pepper.

Wipe the wok clean with kitchen paper, then reheat until very hot. Add the remaining oil. Stir-fry the mangetout and red pepper for about 2 minutes, then add the sherry. Return the beef (with a slotted spoon) to the pan and add the black bean sauce. Toss everything together to heat through, which should take 1–2 minutes.

Cook the noodles according to the packet directions. Drain and season to taste with a dash of sesame oil. Serve with the beef.

# Crab and dill pasta

**If you can find any fresh seaweed (such as dulse), rinse it thoroughly to remove excess salt and toss a handful into the dish towards the end.**

Cook the pasta in boiling salted water until *al dente*. Meanwhile, melt the butter in a saucepan, then add the mascarpone and crabmeat. Heat very gently, stirring, until very warm. Remove from the heat, add the dill and season to taste (do not add salt if you are also adding seaweed).

Drain the pasta, then toss with the crab mixture and serve at once.

### SERVES 4

300g/10½oz linguine or spaghetti

25g/1oz butter

250g/9oz mascarpone cheese

200g/7oz crabmeat (preferably more white meat than brown)

15g/½oz fresh dill, chopped

salt and freshly ground black pepper

# Steak and chips with Roquefort butter

**This recipe is not for *frites,* but for real chips – fat wedges of potato that are soft inside and nicely crisp outside. Use whichever type of fat you prefer, but *aficionados* claim that beef dripping is best of all. Choose a floury maincrop potato such as King Edward, Cara or Maris Piper. Serve with a side salad.**

Make the Roquefort butter by mashing the cheese and butter together with plenty of black pepper until smooth. Spoon on to a piece of foil, shape into a roll and chill. (Use any leftovers to top baked potatoes.)

Peel the potatoes, cut them into thick chips and place in a bowl of cold water until required (this prevents them sticking together during cooking). Pat them thoroughly dry in a clean tea towel before frying.

Put the dripping or vegetable oil in a large deep pan or deep-fat fryer, filling it no more than half full. Heat to 180°C/350°F. If you have no thermometer, drop in a tester chip: it should sizzle in a mass of tiny bubbles. Lower in the potatoes in a wire basket (or tip them straight in, then remove with a slotted spoon). Cook for 5–6 minutes and then drain on kitchen paper. Increase the temperature to 190°C/375°F: a tester chip will turn golden brown in less than 1 minute. Fry the chips again for about 3 minutes or until golden brown and crisp. Drain on kitchen paper and season generously with salt.

During the first stage of chip-frying, heat a heavy frying pan to hot. Season the steaks with salt and pepper. Add the sunflower oil to the pan and, once smoking, add the steaks and cook for 2–3 minutes on each side, or until cooked to your liking. To prevent the steaks sticking to the base, do not touch them until 2 minutes is up.

Serve the steaks on warmed plates topped with a thin pat of chilled Roquefort butter and accompanied by a pile of chips.

### SERVES 2

25g/1oz Roquefort cheese, crumbled

40g/1½oz unsalted butter, softened

2 large floury potatoes

dripping or vegetable oil for frying

2 steaks (rump, sirloin or rib-eye)

2 tablespoons sunflower oil

salt and freshly ground black pepper

# Beetroot and red wine risotto

**SERVES 4**

3 tablespoons olive oil

1 onion, chopped

2 celery sticks, chopped

250g/9oz arborio rice

150ml/5fl oz red wine

600ml/1 pint hot vegetable or chicken stock

175g/6oz cooked (not pickled) beetroot, diced

3 tablespoons chopped fresh dill

1 tablespoon extra virgin olive oil

salt and freshly ground black pepper

freshly grated Parmesan cheese, to serve

**Even if you are convinced you detest beetroot, do try this. Its pungent flavour is sweetened by fresh dill and the resulting taste is a million miles away from the hideous, vinegary beetroot that used to be dumped on plates of cold meat with grey-tinged hard-boiled egg and tired potato salad. Use a good gutsy wine – anything that you are happy to quaff.**

Heat the oil in a heavy-based saucepan, add the onion and celery and cook gently for 5–10 minutes. Add the rice and stir well to coat with the oil. Add the red wine, bring to the boil and bubble for a couple of minutes, then reduce the heat and gradually add the hot stock: do this a ladleful at a time, allowing each ladleful of stock to be completely absorbed before adding more. After 15 minutes stir in the beetroot and dill, then continue adding stock until the rice is tender – the whole dish should take no more than 30 minutes to cook.

Season to taste with salt and pepper and then stir in the extra virgin oil. Cover and leave for 5 minutes. Serve straight from the pan, sprinkled with grated Parmesan cheese.

# Chicken with a coriander and walnut crust and fried capers

**SERVES 6**

6 boneless free-range chicken breasts, skinned

about 100ml/3½fl oz extra virgin olive oil, plus extra for brushing

40g/1½oz fresh coriander leaves

100g/3½oz walnuts, chopped

65g/2½oz Parmesan cheese, freshly grated

salt and freshly ground black pepper

**For the fried capers:**

1 tablespoon olive oil

100g/3½oz capers, rinsed and patted dry

1 teaspoon balsamic vinegar

**You could substitute pistachios for the walnuts, and plump rabbit joints for the chicken. Serve with the pan juices, some pappardelle pasta and a green salad.**

Put the chicken breasts on a lightly oiled baking sheet, brush with olive oil and season with salt and pepper. Place the coriander leaves in a food processor with the walnuts and cheese. Process briefly, then slowly add enough oil through the feeder tube to form a thickish paste. Season to taste with salt and pepper. Spread a spoonful of the coriander paste over the top of each chicken breast, ensuring it is completely covered. Roast in an oven preheated to 200°C/400°F/Gas Mark 6 for about 20 minutes or until the juices run clear when a skewer is inserted into the fleshiest part.

Just before serving, fry the capers: heat the oil in a frying pan over a high heat, then add the capers and stand back: they will splutter. Cook for 2–3 minutes until they begin to crisp up. Remove from the heat and stir in the vinegar. Pour the capers over the cooked chicken, with the pan juices.

# Tuna, artichoke and mushroom cobbler

## SERVES 4

2 tablespoons olive oil

3 celery sticks, chopped

1 onion, chopped

1 tablespoon chopped fresh tarragon

2 tablespoons plain flour

200ml/7fl oz hot chicken stock

50ml/2fl oz dry white wine or dry vermouth

150ml/5fl oz single cream

grated zest and juice of 1 lemon

200g/7oz mushrooms, roughly chopped

25g/1oz butter

2 x 200g tins of tuna, well drained

260g jar of artichokes in oil, well drained

salt and freshly ground black pepper

### For the cobbler topping:

150g/5½oz plain flour

1 heaped teaspoon baking powder

¼ teaspoon salt

2 tablespoons extra virgin olive oil

1 egg, beaten

50ml/2fl oz milk

**This is a yummy combination of tuna, artichokes and mushrooms under a lemon and tarragon sauce, topped with light olive oil scones. It is fairly filling, so should be accompanied only by some green vegetables or a salad. Be sure to drain the tuna and artichokes very well or you will end up with an oily puddle in the base of the dish.**

Heat the oil in a saucepan, add the celery and onion and fry gently for about 5 minutes, then stir in the tarragon. Add the flour and cook for 1 minute, stirring, then add the hot stock, wine or vermouth and cream. Cook, stirring constantly, for about 4–5 minutes, until thickened. Season with salt and pepper, then stir in the lemon zest and juice. Remove from the heat.

In a separate pan, cook the mushrooms in the butter for about 5 minutes, until tender. Spoon the drained tuna into a 1.5 litre/2½ pint ovenproof dish. Top with the mushrooms and the drained artichokes. Spoon over the sauce and smooth the surface.

Now make the cobbler topping: sift the flour, baking powder and salt into a mixing bowl. Make a well in the centre and add the oil, egg and milk. Using a wooden spoon, mix gently to a soft dough. Do not beat.

Using 2 spoons, drop 4 spoonfuls of the mixture on to the sauce (take a spoonful of the mixture and scrape it off with the other spoon). Place at once in an oven preheated to 220°C/425°F/Gas Mark 7 and bake for about 20 minutes, or until the cobbler topping is risen and golden brown and the filling is piping hot. Serve at once.

# Pasta risotto

Risotto purists would hold up their hands in horror at this recipe. For it uses macaroni instead of rice to make risotto: the pasta is coated in the oil, then hot stock gradually added to the pan, just as if it were a normal risotto made with arborio rice.

Although you can vary the flavourings, I like this version made with sun-dried tomatoes, basil, Parma ham and Parmesan. Because it is cooked in stock rather than water, the pasta takes on a completely different taste. I love it. But it would be tricky to convince an Italian to try it.

Heat the oil in a large pan and add the macaroni. Cook for 2–3 minutes, stirring constantly to coat in the oil. Stir in the sun-dried tomatoes. Add a ladleful of the hot stock, then, once it has all been absorbed, add another ladleful. Continue adding more ladlefuls as the stock is absorbed, stirring often. It should take about 20 minutes in all. You will probably not need all the stock. Season to taste, then remove from the heat. Stir in the basil and Parma ham. Leave to stand for 2–3 minutes, then stir in the Parmesan and serve at once.

## SERVES 4–6

4 tablespoons olive oil (from the jar of tomatoes)

500g/1lb 2oz short-cut macaroni

2 tablespoons sun-dried tomatoes in olive oil, drained and roughly chopped

about 1.7 litres/2¾ pints hot chicken or vegetable stock

1 tablespoon fresh basil leaves, roughly torn

85g/3oz Parma ham, cut into slivers

50g/1¾oz Parmesan cheese, freshly grated

salt and freshly ground black pepper

# Chicken, aubergine and aïoli sandwich

Not exactly something you can grab between your hands and devour standing up, but a truly satisfying sandwich nonetheless. The outer layers are fried slices of aubergine and the filling tender pieces of chicken doused in a garlicky mayonnaise. Since after-work cooking time is too short to make your own mayonnaise, just use a commercial one, to produce a really very acceptable aïoli. Serve with a rocket salad dressed in olive oil and a dash of balsamic vinegar.

Slice the chicken breasts in half horizontally, giving 4 escalopes. Sandwich these between 2 sheets of clingfilm and beat them out to make them thinner.

Heat 1 tablespoon of the oil in a heavy frying pan and fry the aubergine slices until tender and golden brown (about 4 minutes per side), then drain on kitchen paper. Heat the remaining oil in the pan, add the chicken and fry for 2–3 minutes on each side, until cooked through. Season well.

Mix together the mayonnaise, garlic, lemon juice and plenty of salt and pepper. To assemble the sandwiches, place a warm aubergine slice on each plate. Smear over some aïoli, then top with the chicken. Smear over some more aïoli, then cover with the remaining aubergine slice. Serve at once.

## SERVES 2

2 boneless free-range chicken breasts, skinned

2–3 tablespoons olive oil

1 large aubergine, cut lengthways into 4 slices

2 heaped tablespoons mayonnaise

1 large garlic clove, crushed

1 teaspoon lemon juice

salt and freshly ground black pepper

# Tomato and pesto clafoutis

## SERVES 3–4

400g/14oz firm plum tomatoes, thickly sliced

1 heaped teaspoon pesto sauce

2 teaspoons extra virgin olive oil

3 large eggs

100ml/3½ fl oz double cream

100ml/3½ fl oz milk

40g/1½oz plain flour, sifted

40g/1½oz freshly grated Parmesan cheese

salt and freshly ground black pepper

**This is a savoury version of the famous French batter pudding from the Limousin area of France, which is usually made with cherries or plums. It is not dissimilar to toad-in-the-hole, but uses tomatoes and a touch of pesto instead of bangers. Serve warm, with a little salad and some bread.**

Arrange the tomato slices in a lightly oiled 22cm/8¾in gratin dish and season well with salt and pepper. Thin down the pesto with the oil and drizzle it over the tomatoes.

Whisk together all the remaining ingredients, seasoning generously with salt and pepper. Pour this over the tomatoes, then bake immediately in an oven preheated to 220°C/425°F/Gas Mark 7 for 30 minutes, until puffed up and golden brown. Serve at once.

# Hawker's spicy noodles

## SERVES 4

2 teaspoons vegetable oil

250g/9oz lean minced pork

2 garlic cloves, chopped

500ml/18fl oz chicken stock

3 tablespoons dark soy sauce

1 tablespoon rice vinegar

1 teaspoon sesame oil

1–2 red chillies, deseeded and chopped

250g/9oz Chinese wheat noodles

1 tablespoon fresh coriander leaves

1 tablespoon spring onions, chopped

**This dish was inspired by a trip I made recently to the Great Wall of China. At the foot of the long winding steps down from the Wall, past vendors selling silks, pearls and ginger jars, I watched a hawker making noodles. He pulled off a lump of glossy dough, floured it, stretched it, rotated it in the air and slapped it on to the table to knead. Then came the miracle: after a couple of twists, he 'hand-pulled' the dough into fistfuls of long fine noodles, deftly separating the strands with astonishingly rapid fingers. No knife or pasta machine was required, just dexterity and years of practice.**

Heat the oil in a wok and, once it is very hot, add the pork and garlic and fry for about 5 minutes, until the pork is cooked and well browned. Set aside.

Heat the stock in a saucepan with the soy sauce, vinegar, sesame oil and chilli. Bring to the boil and simmer for about 5 minutes.

Cook the noodles according to the packet instructions, then drain well. Tip them into a warm serving bowl, pour over the stock, then top with the pork. Tear the coriander leaves and scatter them over the top, with the spring onions. Serve at once.

# Mushroom pizza

Not really a pizza at all, this is a large flat mushroom base with a topping of the usual pizza accessories – anchovies, tomato, olives and mozzarella. It is quick to prepare and even quicker to devour. Add other toppings such as salami, chicken, prawns or cockles, bolognese sauce or ham, depending on the contents of your larder and refrigerator.

Cut out the stalk of each mushroom and discard (or add to a bolognese sauce). Place the mushrooms on a baking tray and drizzle over a little oil. Bake in an oven preheated to 180°C/350°F/Gas Mark 4 for 15–20 minutes or until tender to the point of a knife. Remove from the oven and increase the temperature to 200°C/400°F/Gas Mark 6. Drain off any excess liquid from the baking tray.

Smear a teaspoon of tomato paste over each mushroom, then top with the cheese. Criss-criss a couple of anchovy pieces over the cheese and top with the olive halves. Tear the oregano over the top and drizzle a teaspoon of oil over each mushroom. Season with plenty of black pepper and bake for about 10 minutes, until the cheese is melted. Eat at once.

**SERVES 2**

4 large flat mushrooms

olive oil

4 teaspoons sun-dried tomato paste

75g/2¾oz mozzarella cheese, grated

4 anchovy fillets, cut lengthways in half

8 black olives, stoned and halved

1 heaped tablespoon fresh oregano

freshly ground black pepper

# Feta, mangetout and olive crumble

Serve this either as a main-course vegetarian dish or as an elaborate accompaniment to roast meat. I prefer to use the authentic Greek or Cypriot feta, which is fairly dry in texture, rather than the creamier French feta.

Blanch the mangetout in boiling water for about 30 seconds, then drain and refresh in cold water to retain their colour. Pat dry.

Arrange half the tomato slices in a 1.2 litre/2 pint ovenproof dish, top with the mangetout and season well. Top with the remaining tomato slices, season, then scatter over the olives.

For the crumble topping, mix together the feta and breadcrumbs. Rub in the butter, then stir in the tarragon and mustard. Season with pepper but not salt, as the feta will be salty. Tip this mixture over the vegetables and press down. Drizzle over the oil. Bake in an oven preheated to 180°C/ 350°F/Gas Mark 4 for about 30 minutes or until the topping is golden brown and crunchy.

**SERVES 3–4 AS A MAIN COURSE, 4–6 AS AN ACCOMPANIMENT**

200g/7oz mangetout, halved

4 plum tomatoes, thickly sliced

75g/2¾oz black olives, stoned

1 tablespoon olive oil

salt and freshly ground black pepper

**For the crumble topping:**

100g/3½oz feta cheese, crumbled or roughly grated

75g/2¾oz Granary breadcrumbs

50g/1¾oz unsalted butter, diced

1 tablespoon chopped fresh tarragon

½ teaspoon mustard powder

**Y**ou either love them or hate them. Picnics are the mainstay of many families; others never bother with them. I am an unashamed picnic lover and so I don't really understand those who insist they can't be doing with sandy sandwiches, howling gales and billowing wind-breaks. Admittedly it's not exactly a glamorous meal and never rates among life's most sophisticated. But it can still be truly memorable, even from a culinary point of view, and there is always plenty of opportunity for fun.

Barbecues fall into the same category. And here I must confess I used to hate them, although I could never pin down exactly why. Perhaps the entire macho male spectacle, where men speared slabs of meat and cooked them until burnt outside, raw inside, seemed simply too prehistoric. There was also the predictability of it all. There were invariably burgers and sausages, an undressed salad, and corn on the cob that only the dentally unchallenged could get their teeth round. But gradually – probably during my stay in Australia – I became aware of the endless possibilities of the barbecue. Fish, vegetables and all sorts of meat, poultry and game can be cooked over the coals. I have even come to accept the statutory male-chef role of barbecue culture. Just as long as they also do the washing up.

# CHAPTER SEVEN
# picnics and barbecues

# Chargrilled chicken and tapenade on sourdough

**SERVES 4**

| |
|---|
| 4 large boneless free-range chicken breasts, skinned |
| 3 tablespoons olive oil |
| juice of 1 large lemon |
| 8 thick slices of sourdough bread |
| 185g jar of black olive tapenade |
| 4–5 plum tomatoes, sliced |
| salt and freshly ground black pepper |

**Instead of grilling the chicken you could barbecue it for a nicely smoky flavour. Begin preparing this tasty sandwich the day before your picnic.**

Place the chicken breasts between sheets of clingfilm and roll with a rolling pin (or beat with a meat mallet). Unwrap and place in a large shallow dish. Pour over the oil and lemon juice and add plenty of freshly ground black pepper. Turn the chicken over, then cover and leave for 2–3 hours.

Heat a griddle pan (or a heavy frying pan) without oil until it is extremely hot. Remove the chicken from the marinade and cook on the griddle for 2–3 minutes on each side, until nicely charred and just cooked through. Transfer to a plate, season generously with salt and then leave to cool.

Cut each breast into 3–4 pieces. Thickly spread the bread with tapenade. Distribute the chicken over 4 of the slices and top with the tomatoes. Season, then sandwich together with the remaining bread. Press down gently, cut in half, then wrap in foil. Place in the fridge, weighted down, overnight.

Next day, take the sandwiches on your picnic and unwrap. Arm yourselves with napkins and devour messily.

# Smoked salmon and cucumber sandwich loaf

**SERVES 8**

| |
|---|
| 1 small cucumber |
| 1 teaspoon white wine vinegar |
| 450g/1lb wholemeal or light rye loaf |
| 200g/7oz cream cheese, softened |
| 250–275g/9–9½oz smoked salmon |
| 2 tablespoons chopped fresh chives |
| salt |

**This is based on a Finnish recipe, *voileipakakku* – a more elaborate sandwich loaf: alternate layers of rye and white bread sandwiched with egg, ham and cheese butters, then decorated with mayonnaise and pieces of olive, gherkin and tomato. My version is simpler but no less delicious. Take a sharp knife for cutting or slice the loaf at home first.**

Peel the cucumber with a vegetable peeler, then slice thinly. Place in a bowl with 3 teaspoons of salt and the wine vinegar. Turn everything together, then leave for a couple of hours. Rinse in a colander and pat dry with a tea towel.

Using a sharp bread knife, cut thin slices from the top and base of the loaf and discard. Cut the loaf lengthways into 6 slices, about 1cm/½in thick.

Place the first slice on a board and spread thickly with cream cheese, then add a third of the smoked salmon. Sprinkle liberally with chives, then put a second slice of bread on top and spread with more cream cheese. Top with cucumber slices and season well. Continue these layers, then spread the last slice with the remaining cream cheese and place on top (plain side uppermost). Press down firmly – but not too vigorously, otherwise the fillings will escape. Wrap tightly in foil, weight down and refrigerate for 24 hours. Next day, remove the foil, cut off the crusts around the sides and cut the loaf into 8 slices.

# Barbecued mushrooms with anchovy mayonnaise

**Be sure to light the barbecue well ahead of cooking: at least three-quarters of the charcoal should be covered by a greyish ash.**

**If by any chance the heavens open shortly before you are ready to cook, just bake the mushrooms in a hot oven until tender – at least 30 minutes, depending on thickness.**

Whizz the mayonnaise, anchovies and garlic together in a food processor and then chill until required. Wipe the mushrooms, then brush generously with olive oil. Grill for 4–5 minutes on each side, until tender, then season with salt and pepper.

To serve, dollop mayonnaise on to a mushroom and eat warm.

**SERVES 8**

200g/7oz (about 5 tablespoons) mayonnaise

4 anchovy fillets

1 garlic clove, crushed

8 large flat mushrooms

olive oil for brushing

salt and freshly ground black pepper

To test the heat of the barbecue, hold your hand palm down a couple of inches above the coals: if you can withstand the heat for more than 4 seconds it is not hot enough; 2 seconds is hot enough.

# Courgette and mint tortilla

**One of Spain's most popular dishes, tortilla is classically a thick onion and potato omelette. Served cold, it is perfect picnic fare. Served warm, it makes ideal tapas, with huge jugs of fruity sangria.**

Heat the oil in a heavy pan suitable for both hob and oven (mine is cast-iron, 25cm/10in in diameter and 5cm/2in deep). Cook the onion in the oil for about 3 minutes, then add the diced potatoes and cook, stirring occasionally, for about 10 minutes or until they are tender. Add the courgettes and fry for a further 4–5 minutes, stirring to coat in the oil.

Beat the eggs, mint, salt and plenty of black pepper together and pour this mixture over the vegetables (do remember when adding the salt and pepper that cold food requires more seasoning than hot). Remove the pan from the heat and place in an oven preheated to 180°C/350°F/Gas Mark 4 for 30–35 minutes, until the tortilla is set and golden brown. Loosen around the edges with a knife and allow to cool before turning out on to foil. Cut into wedges and eat warm or cold.

**SERVES 6**

3 tablespoons olive oil

1 onion, chopped

600g/1lb 5oz potatoes, peeled and finely diced

400g/14oz courgettes, diced

6 medium eggs

2 tablespoons chopped fresh mint

1 teaspoon salt

freshly ground black pepper

# Granary picnic loaf with salami and grilled peppers

**SERVES 8**

1 yellow, 1 orange and 2 red peppers

1 large round Granary loaf

about 2 tablespoons pesto sauce

100g/3½oz salami

40g/1½oz rocket

2 tablespoons olive oil, plus extra for brushing

2 tablespoons chopped sun-dried tomatoes

2 tablespoons torn fresh basil leaves

salt and freshly ground black pepper

**This is yet another messy dish – perfect for the great outdoors. Be sure to begin preparing it the night before your picnic. You could substitute vegetables such as asparagus, artichokes or courgettes for the peppers and feta, goat's cheese or tinned sardines for the salami.**

Halve and deseed the peppers, then grill them until charred and blackened. Wrap in foil so the steam will loosen the skin.

Cut the lid off the loaf and remove most of the inside, leaving thick walls. Brush a little oil around the cavity and the lid, then smear with a thin layer of pesto.

Skin the peppers and slice them into slivers. Pack half of these into the loaf, then top with half the salami and half the rocket. Pour over 1 tablespoon of the oil, season generously, then top with the sun-dried tomatoes and basil. Add the remaining peppers, salami and rocket, season again and drizzle with the remaining oil. Pack down the fillings and replace the lid. Wrap tightly in foil and leave in the refrigerator overnight. Serve cut into wedges.

## A family picnic

**Chargrilled chicken and tapenade on sourdough**    100

**Granary picnic loaf with salami and grilled peppers**

**Tortilla hot dogs**    104

**Caramel toffee flapjack** 187

## Joanna's wine notes

Unless you are anticipating an icy picnic, take a red that tastes good lightly chilled – a Barbera d'Asti, Sancerre or Beaujolais (or almost any of the very cheapest red wines). Alternatively, refresh a hot summer's day with a juicy, dry rosé such as a Bordeaux, Vin de Pays d'Oc or Australian Grenache.

# Spinach empanadas

**MAKES 10**

| |
|---|
| 300g/10½oz strong white flour |
| 1 heaped teaspoon easy-blend dried yeast |
| 2 tablespoons olive oil, plus extra for brushing |
| 150–175ml/5–6fl oz lukewarm water |
| 200g/7oz fresh spinach |
| 4 garlic cloves, chopped |
| 75g/2¾oz cheese, grated |
| salt and freshly ground black pepper |

**If possible, use a mixture of manchego (a Spanish ewe's milk cheese) and Parmesan in the filling of these little turnovers; otherwise a mature Cheddar will do.**

Mix the flour, yeast and ½ teaspoon of salt in a bowl. Add 1 tablespoon of the oil and just enough lukewarm water to form a stiff dough. Turn out on to a floured board and knead for 5–10 minutes, until smooth. Place in a lightly oiled bowl, cover and leave somewhere warm for about 1 hour, until risen.

Heat the remaining oil in a saucepan, add the spinach and garlic and cook for about 3 minutes, until the spinach has wilted. Drain thoroughly, then chop. Place in a bowl, season well and stir in the cheese. Leave to cool.

Knock back the dough and knead it lightly for a minute or two. Divide it into 10 pieces and roll out each piece into a circle about 13–14cm/5–5½in in diameter. Divide the spinach mixture between the circles, placing it on one half of each one. Fold over (pasty-like) and crimp the edges to seal. Place on an oiled baking tray and brush the tops with a little olive oil. Leave, uncovered, for about 20 minutes, then bake in an oven preheated to 220°C/425°F/Gas Mark 7 for about 15 minutes, until golden brown. Leave until cold before packing to take on your picnic.

# Tortilla hot dogs

**SERVES 8**

| |
|---|
| 8 large or 16 regular frankfurters |
| 8 large, soft flour tortillas |
| mild mustard, to serve |

**Optional extras:**

| |
|---|
| grated cheese |
| soured cream |
| chopped lettuce |

**The ideal medium for cooking the frankfurters in this recipe is a bonfire. The same principle applies to bonfires as to barbecues: don't start cooking until the fire has burned down and the glowing embers are covered with grey ash. A medium-sized bonfire will take a good 30 minutes to reach this temperature.**

**If you don't have a bonfire (or if they are banned at your picnic site), then use a barbecue or, if you are really in fanatical camping mode, set up a primus stove and simmer the sausages in a pan of water.**

Heat the frankfurters over a bonfire, barbecue or primus stove until piping hot. Wrap the tortillas loosely in foil and warm them gently over the embers of the fire (or over a barbecue or over the steam of the pan).

To serve, generously smear the warm tortillas with mustard, add the optional ingredients, if using, and place 1 or 2 hot dogs in the middle. Roll the tortilla around the frankfurters and devour while hot.

# Stuffed spicy sea bass

I was given a variation on this recipe at the home of Edinburgh-based Indian cookery teacher Sunanda Banham. Although she makes her own paneer, you can now thankfully buy reasonable paneer in supermarkets and Indian food shops. If you cannot find it, however, use mozzarella as a substitute.

Instead of the sea bass, sea trout is also good.

Heat 1 tablespoon of the oil in a pan, add the onions and fry until softened. Place the onions in a blender with the remaining oil, the spices, ginger, yoghurt, tomatoes, garlic and a teaspoon of salt. Blend to a fine purée. Mix 2 tablespoons of the purée with the spring onions, paneer and a pinch of salt and set aside. Pour the rest of the purée over the fish, cover and marinate for at least 4 hours (or overnight).

Use the paneer mixture to stuff the fish, sealing the opening with a strip of foil. Secure the fish in a fish grill, if you have one, and barbecue for about 15 minutes on each side, basting occasionally with the remaining marinade.

## SERVES 4

| |
|---|
| 165ml/5½fl oz vegetable oil |
| 2 red onions, chopped |
| ¾ teaspoon ground turmeric |
| ¾ teaspoon cayenne pepper |
| ½ teaspoon ground cumin |
| 1cm/½in cinnamon stick |
| 1½ teaspoons coriander seeds |
| 3 cardamom pods |
| 1 tablespoon freshly grated root ginger |
| 2 tablespoons natural yoghurt |
| 2 tablespoons chopped tomatoes |
| 1 garlic clove, peeled |
| 4–6 spring onions, chopped |
| 100g/3½oz paneer, grated |
| 1 x 900g/2lb sea bass, boned and scaled from the back |
| salt |

# Beetroot and ginger chutney

This chutney has a gloriously rich colour and is spiced with fresh ginger and peppercorns. If you wear thin plastic household gloves to peel and grate the beetroot, you won't be walking around with purple fingernails for the next three days.

The chutney is perfect to take on picnics, as an accompaniment to cheese, cold meats and pies.

Grate the beetroot and put it in a large preserving pan with all the other ingredients. Stir well, bring slowly to the boil, then reduce the heat slightly; it should be something between a simmer and a fierce boil. Cook, uncovered, for about 1½ hours or until thick, stirring frequently to prevent burning at the base. Pot at once in warm sterilized jars and seal either immediately or when completely cold. Label and store in a cool, dark place.

## MAKES 2.7kg/6lb

| |
|---|
| 1.1kg/2½lb raw beetroot (peeled weight) |
| 450g/1lb onions, chopped |
| 450g/1lb cooking apples, peeled, cored and chopped |
| 450g/1lb raisins |
| 900g/2lb granulated sugar |
| 1.2 litres/2 pints distilled malt vinegar |
| 2–3 heaped tablespoons freshly grated root ginger |
| 1 heaped tablespoon black peppercorns |
| 1 teaspoon salt |

# Marinated tuna with roasted tomato relish

## SERVES 4

4 thick tuna steaks (about 175g/
6oz each)

1 red chilli, finely chopped

juice of 1 lime

5 tablespoons olive oil

2 tablespoons chopped fresh basil

2 tablespoons chopped fresh
coriander

6 plum tomatoes, halved

salt and freshly ground black pepper

**Thick, succulent tuna steaks are first marinated in a simple dressing, then barbecued until just cooked. They are served with a warm roasted tomato relish flavoured with basil and coriander.**

Place the tuna steaks in a non-metallic bowl. Mix together the chilli, lime juice, 4 tablespoons of the olive oil and 1 tablespoon each of the basil and coriander. Season with plenty of black pepper and pour over the tuna. Leave for up to 2 hours, stirring gently once.

For the relish, arrange the tomatoes on a lightly oiled baking tray and pour over the remaining olive oil. Place in an oven preheated to 220°C/425°F/Gas Mark 7 for about 30 minutes, or until they are soft and juicy and slightly caramelized, then remove the tray from the oven and tip the contents into a saucepan.

Remove the tuna from the marinade and barbecue for 2–3 minutes on each side, seasoning with a little salt and pepper. Pour the marinade into the saucepan containing the roast tomatoes and bring slowly to the boil. Once it is bubbling, boil for 1 minute, then remove from the heat and stir in the remaining chopped basil and coriander. Taste and check the seasoning, then serve with the tuna steaks.

> Oil the grill lightly with vegetable oil before cooking fish on a barbecue, to prevent sticking.

## A barbecue party

**Barbecued mushrooms
with anchovy
mayonnaise**                     101

**Marinated tuna with
roasted tomato relish**

**Algerian guinea fowl
with avocado relish**         109

**Black bean and red
pepper salad**                      44

## Joanna's wine notes

A ripe, spicy red wine is essential; a Californian Zinfandel or Australian Shiraz would hit the spot. If you're serving white as well, choose one with plenty of oomph. There is always Chardonnay but Australian Semillon, Marsanne or Verdelho would make a change.

# Spicy chicken kebabs

**SERVES 4–6**

| |
|---|
| 4 large boneless free-range chicken breasts, skinned |
| 200ml/7fl oz Greek yoghurt |
| 2 teaspoons freshly grated root ginger |
| 2 garlic cloves, crushed |
| juice of 1 lemon |
| 1 tablespoon sunflower oil |
| 1 tablespoon ground coriander |
| 2 teaspoons ground cumin |
| ½ teaspoon cayenne pepper |
| ½ teaspoon paprika |
| ¼ teaspoon salt |
| 15g/½oz fresh coriander, chopped |

**These make wonderful barbecue food as they are loved by both adults and children. Cook them under a regular grill if the rain clouds gather. To serve them as canapés, use smaller 'satay' sticks.**

Cut the chicken into large dice and place in a bowl. Mix together all the remaining ingredients and pour them over the chicken. Stir gently, cover and refrigerate for at least 6 hours or overnight.

The next day, thread the chicken on to wooden skewers that have been soaked in water for 30 minutes (this helps prevent them burning). Cook either on a barbecue or under a grill for 10–15 minutes, turning, until cooked through. Serve with naan bread and salad

# Bush bread with beer

**MAKES 1 LOAF OR 8–10 DAMPERS**

| |
|---|
| 450g/1lb self-raising flour, sifted |
| 1 heaped teaspoon caster sugar |
| 1 heaped teaspoon salt |
| 8–10 tablespoons beer and water, mixed |

**This Australian bread is cooked in the outback and is similar to damper bread, which is simply a flour, salt and water dough twisted around a green stick and cooked over bonfire embers. These are the ones we cook on picnics and I usually mix the dough at home first, but you could also mix it *in situ*. (My husband Pat is a green stick expert – he would have been a good Boy Scout – and is to be seen at our lochside picnic sites whittling away sticks with a sturdy penknife.)**

**Another variation is to knead the dough into a ball and place it at the side of the fire to cook. Even if still slightly doughy inside, it tastes like the best bread you have ever eaten. It is true what they say about the great outdoors – everything tastes better.**

Mix together the flour, sugar and salt. Add enough beer/water to make a fairly stiff dough. Knead gently, then place in a lightly greased camp oven (or deep tin) and cover with a lid, making sure there is a little space for rising. Bury in hot campfire ashes and leave for about 1 hour or until cooked.

For dampers, wrap pieces of the dough around green sticks. Hold the sticks over the glowing embers and cook for 5–8 minutes, turning frequently. Serve with butter and golden syrup, honey or jam.

# Algerian guinea fowl with avocado relish

**After being marinated with North African-style spices, the guinea fowl can be cooked either in a conventional oven or over a barbecue. Serve with baked sweet potatoes.**

Place the guinea fowl in a non-metallic dish. Combine the garlic, ginger, fennel seeds, saffron, spring onions, paprika and oil with ¼ teaspoon of cayenne pepper and 75ml/3fl oz of lemon juice. Stir in all but 1 tablespoon of the coriander and plenty of black pepper. Pour over the fowl and marinate for at least 6 hours or overnight.

If you are using a barbecue, cook the guinea fowl for about 20 minutes per 450g/1lb (depending on the heat of your barbecue), loosely wrapped in foil for the first 20 minutes; baste the birds a couple of times with the remaining marinade.

If you are cooking them in the oven, place the unwrapped fowl in a roasting tin, pour over the marinade and sprinkle with some salt. Roast at 220°C/425°F/Gas Mark 7 for 15 minutes, then reduce the oven temperature to 190°C/375°F/Gas Mark 5 and cook for a further 20 minutes per 450g/1lb. Check the birds are cooked through (same test for barbecue and oven) by piercing the thickest part of the flesh: the juices should run clear. Leave to rest for 10 minutes.

Meanwhile, make the relish: put the avocados in a food processor with ¼ teaspoon of salt, a pinch of cayenne pepper, 1½ tablespoons of lemon juice and the remaining chopped coriander. Process until combined but still chunky. Check the seasoning.

Serve a dollop of the avocado relish with the carved guinea fowl (and the pan juices if you roasted them in the oven).

## SERVES 4

|  |
| --- |
| 2 guinea fowl |
| 2 garlic cloves, chopped |
| 1 tablespoon freshly grated root ginger |
| 1 tablespoon fennel seeds |
| ½ teaspoon saffron strands |
| 4 spring onions, chopped |
| 1 teaspoon paprika |
| 150ml/5fl oz olive oil |
| cayenne pepper |
| lemon juice |
| 15g/½oz fresh coriander, chopped |
| 2 ripe avocados, peeled, stoned and chopped |
| salt and freshly ground black pepper |

# Barbecued mussels in foil

Having always enjoyed surprises, I have to admit I love serving these packages of delicious goodies. The mussels are cooked in foil on the barbecue then opened up at the table to release a fabulous 'eat-me' aroma. Once you have forked out all the plump, tender mussels, arm yourself with plenty of bread to dunk into the juices captured in the foil.

You will need 24 large mussels but it is a good idea to buy about 30 or so, just in case any are damaged or open.

Cut four 30cm/12in squares of foil and place on a work surface. Lightly oil them, then divide the first 5 ingredients in a little heap in the middle of the foil. Season with salt and pepper and pour ½ tablespoon of wine over each one. Top with 6 mussels, then pour over ½ tablespoon of oil. Carefully pull up the edges of the foil and crimp together to close them tightly. Place the foil parcels on the hottest part of the barbecue and cook for at least 10 minutes, until the mussels have all opened up (peek inside one parcel to check). To serve, place the parcels on plates so each person can open up their own.

## SERVES 4

2 plum tomatoes, chopped

3 spring onions, chopped

2 heaped tablespoons chopped fresh parsley

2 teaspoons freshly grated root ginger

3 garlic cloves, chopped

2 tablespoons dry white wine

24 large mussels, cleaned

2 tablespoons olive oil

salt and freshly ground black pepper

# Tablet

As a child, I often attended local fairs and fêtes where home-baking, jams and sweets were a speciality. The mark of a good fair was when the cake and candy stall had a mile-long queue, even before the official opening by some visiting dignitary in a flowery hat. Tablet has the consistency of slightly hard fudge and the flavour of buttery toffee. For variety, add grated white chocolate, ginger syrup or coconut at the end.

Melt the butter in a heavy-based saucepan, then add the sugar, milk and salt. Stir well until the sugar has dissolved, then slowly bring to the boil. Simmer for 10 minutes over a fairly high heat, stirring occasionally. Add the condensed milk and simmer for a further 8–10 minutes on a slightly lower heat, so it bubbles but not too fiercely. Cook, stirring constantly, until the mixture reaches the soft-ball stage: this is tested by dropping a little of the mixture into a cup of very cold water. If it can be moulded into a soft ball with your fingers, it is ready. Remove from the heat. Using a hand-held electric beater, beat the mixture for 3–5 minutes (or for 10 minutes by hand). Stir in the vanilla extract, then pour the mixture into a buttered 23 x 33cm/9 x 13in swiss roll tin. Leave to cool, then cut into small squares and pack in an airtight tin – preferably out of (tempting) sight.

## MAKES 50 TINY SQUARES

125g/4½oz unsalted butter

900g/2lb granulated sugar

300ml/10fl oz milk

a pinch of salt

200g/7oz tin of condensed milk

1 teaspoon pure vanilla extract

I can think of few more pleasant things in life than having friends round to supper. Grand dinner parties do, of course, have their merits, but it is only with friends and family that one feels truly relaxed and the meal can be completely informal. Supper with friends can be eaten in the kitchen, provided your kitchen can accommodate more than two diners. The type of food most of us like to cook for friends is really an extension of what the family would normally eat, but with a little more emphasis on detail, both in the food and the table setting. Many dishes can be served in the containers in which they are cooked. And there is usually a starter and perhaps two puddings, depending on numbers.

Cooking for friends means that you can try out a brand-new recipe on them or experiment with some exotic ingredients; or you can rustle up that old favourite, knowing it will be an out-and-out success. Because you know your friends' likes and dislikes you don't have to go down the safe middle route and offer roast and three veg. On the other hand, if you feel in serious need of comfort food, then serve old-fashioned shepherd's pie, fish pie or steamed pudding and watch everyone's face light up in anticipatory delight.

CHAPTER EIGHT

# cooking for friends

# Sweet potato mash with yassa chicken

## SERVES 4

8 free-range chicken pieces

1 tablespoon sherry vinegar

juice of 1 large lime

2 yellow peppers, deseeded and sliced

a large pinch of chilli powder

4 garlic cloves, crushed

3 tablespoons sunflower oil

2 large onions, sliced

salt and freshly ground black pepper

**For the sweet potato mash:**

1kg/2¼lb sweet potatoes

50g/1¾oz butter

1 heaped tablespoon mascarpone cheese (or other cream cheese)

### A winter supper

**Mussels with chilli and coriander**    87

**Sweet potato mash with yassa chicken**

**Pear and cranberry tarte tatin**    179

### Joanna's wine notes

The best wine for the mussels, with their flavourings of chilli, coriander and tomato, is Sauvignon Blanc. A New Zealand Sauvignon has the ripe intensity to cope with the chicken and sweet potatoes as well. However, if you pick a lighter Sauvignon you may want to switch to a richer Viognier or Chardonnay – even a Meursault – with the chicken.

Our friends Dilys and Jimmy now live in Uganda. When they lived in the Gambia they often used to make a local dish, chicken Yassa. Yassa originates in southern Senegal (the Casamance region) and was originally made by the Jola tribe using monkey. I think I'll stick to chicken.

Try to find orange-fleshed sweet potatoes for this recipe. The mascarpone is not essential but it makes the potatoes even more luscious and creamy. The mash can be prepared in advance and reheated, covered in buttered foil.

Place the chicken pieces in a bowl with the vinegar, lime juice, yellow peppers, chilli, garlic and some salt and pepper. Stir gently and leave for about 1 hour. Meanwhile, heat the oil in a large flameproof casserole and fry the onions for 10–15 minutes, until golden brown. Using a slotted spoon, transfer them to a plate.

Remove the chicken pieces from the bowl and brown them all over in the oil (in 2 batches). Add the remaining marinade and the onions (and juices) to the casserole with the chicken, season with salt and pepper and cover tightly with a lid. Bake in an oven preheated to 180°C/350°F/Gas Mark 4 for about 1 hour. Check the seasoning and serve, straight from the casserole, with the sweet potato mash.

For the sweet potato mash, scrub the sweet potatoes and then dry well. Place on a baking tray and bake in an oven preheated to 200°C/400°F/Gas Mark 6 for about 1 hour or until tender. Once they are cool enough to handle, slit each one along the middle and scoop out the lovely soft orange flesh into a bowl. Mash with the butter and mascarpone, adding plenty of salt and pepper to taste. Serve piping hot with the chicken.

# Lamb and quince tagine

A tagine is simply a Moroccan stew of meat or poultry and aromatic spices. Called after the pot in which it is cooked – a round dish with a conical lid – a tagine can be made in any solid casserole dish with a tight-fitting lid. Serve with hot couscous dressed in a little olive oil and some freshly chopped coriander.

If you want to make this simple stew when quinces are out of season, substitute cooking apples or pears.

Heat the oil in a heavy casserole and brown the lamb all over. Transfer to a plate with a slotted spoon, then fry the onion and carrots for about 5 minutes. Increase the heat to high and add all the spices. Stirring continually, fry for 30–40 seconds, then return the meat to the pan and add the hot stock. While it is coming to the boil, peel and core the quince. Cut each into 8 pieces and add to the pan with some salt and pepper. Stir and bring back to the boil, then cover tightly and place in an oven preheated to 150°C/300°F/Gas Mark 2 for about 2 hours, until the quince are soft and the meat tender. Taste for seasoning and serve.

## SERVES 6

2 tablespoons olive oil

1kg/2¼lb shoulder of lamb, cubed

1 large onion, sliced

2 carrots, diced

2 teaspoons ground cumin

1 teaspoon ground cinnamon

1 teaspoon ground ginger

a good pinch of saffron strands

400ml/14fl oz hot lamb stock

2 large quince

salt and freshly ground black pepper

# Fresh tomato and feta penne

An Italian house guest made this for us during his summer stay. He was very particular about the type of cheese – cow's milk mozzarella (he insisted buffalo mozzarella is only for raw dishes) – and used only the ripest tomatoes and the best olive oil. Once he had gone I fiddled around with the recipe and ended up using feta cheese, which adds a welcome tang to this wonderfully summery dish.

Pat the tomatoes dry on kitchen paper. Tip into a large bowl, then season with the salt, sugar and plenty of pepper. Add the garlic and basil. Dice the feta to the same size as the tomatoes and add to the bowl with 6 tablespoons of the oil. Stir well and leave to stand for 2 hours at room temperature, stirring once.

Cook the pasta in plenty of boiling salted water until tender, then drain and return to the hot pan, off the heat. Add the tomato and feta mixture and gently toss everything together, using 2 large spoons. Do this carefully for 3–4 minutes until the cheese just begins to melt. Add an extra tablespoon of oil if it starts to stick. Taste and adjust the seasoning, then serve at once in warm bowls.

## SERVES 6

1kg/2¼lb large tomatoes, deseeded and diced

1 teaspoon salt

½ teaspoon sugar

4 garlic cloves, finely chopped

15g/½oz fresh basil leaves

200g/7oz Greek feta cheese

6–7 tablespoons extra virgin olive oil

600g/1lb 5oz dried penne

freshly ground black pepper

# Venison chilli

**SERVES 6**

2 tablespoons vegetable oil

1 large onion, chopped

3 garlic cloves, chopped

1 red chilli, deseeded and chopped

500g/1lb 2oz venison mince

1 teaspoon freeze-dried oregano

1 teaspoon salt

½ teaspoon ground cumin

1–2 teaspoons chilli powder

150ml/5fl oz tomato passata

420g tin of kidney beans, drained

200ml/7fl oz dark beer (stout)

soured cream, to serve

**This is delicious served with soured cream and baked potatoes or, my favourite, cornbread (see page 72).**

Heat the oil in a large pan, add the onion and fry gently for about 10 minutes, until softened. Add the garlic and chilli and fry for 2–3 minutes. Increase the heat and add the mince, stirring well to break up. Once it is browned all over, stir in the oregano, salt, cumin and chilli powder. Cook for 2 minutes. Stir in the passata, kidney beans and beer, then bring to the boil. Reduce the heat to a low simmer, cover and cook for about 1½ hours. Taste for seasoning and serve piping hot, with a spoonful of soured cream on top of each portion.

# Herring gratin

**SERVES 6**

1.25kg/2¾lb large potatoes

15g/½oz butter

1 onion, finely chopped

2 garlic cloves, chopped

6 large herring fillets, skinned and halved lengthways

600ml/1 pint single cream

2 tablespoons wholegrain mustard

25g/1oz fresh breadcrumbs

1 tablespoon olive oil

salt and freshly ground black pepper

**This recipe is loosely based on a much-loved Swedish recipe, Jansson's Temptation, which is a gratin of potatoes, anchovies and cream. I like to use herring fillets and add some wholegrain mustard, which complements the fish perfectly.**

**For speed and ease, ask your fishmonger to skin the herring fillets for you. Serve the gratin with a crisp green salad.**

Peel the potatoes and cut them into very thin slices (I use my food processor). Melt the butter in a small pan and gently fry the onion and garlic for 2–3 minutes, until softened. Arrange half the potatoes in a large buttered gratin dish, seasoning well with salt and pepper. Next, tip the onion, garlic and butter all over them. Arrange the herrings on top, trying not to overlap them. Season again, then top with the rest of the potatoes. Season again. Mix the cream and mustard together and pour slowly over the dish, ensuring all the potatoes are covered. Cover the dish with buttered foil and cook in an oven preheated to 200°C/400°F/Gas Mark 6 for 45 minutes. Remove the foil, sprinkle over the breadcrumbs and drizzle with the oil. Return to the oven for 45–50 minutes or until the potatoes are completely soft. Leave to rest for at least 10 minutes before serving.

# Meatloaf with roasted hazelnut and tomato sauce

## SERVES 6

450g/1lb lean minced beef

250g/9oz lean minced pork

75g/2¾oz fresh breadcrumbs

1 medium egg

½ large onion, finely chopped

1 tablespoon Worcestershire sauce

1 tablespoon chopped fresh coriander

salt and freshly ground black pepper

**For the sauce:**

2 large (beef) tomatoes

2 garlic cloves, peeled but left whole

1 red chilli, halved and deseeded

100g/3½oz blanched hazelnuts

4 tablespoons olive oil

1 tablespoon sherry vinegar

1 heaped tablespoon chopped fresh coriander

**Any leftover meatloaf is good cold the next day, with chutney or pickles. Serve with new potatoes and green vegetables.**

For the meatloaf, combine everything in a bowl, seasoning well with salt and pepper. Spoon the mixture into a lightly buttered 1kg/2¼lb loaf tin, pressing well down. Cover loosely with foil and bake in an oven preheated to 150°C/300°F/Gas Mark 2 for 1¾–2 hours. Remove from the oven and leave to cool for at least 20 minutes, then carefully drain away any liquid and turn out the meatloaf.

For the sauce, cut each tomato into 4 thick slices and place on a baking tray with the garlic cloves, chilli and hazelnuts. Drizzle over half the oil and place in an oven preheated to 190°C/375°F/Gas Mark 5 for 20–25 minutes or until the vegetables are soft. Tip everything carefully into a blender or liquidizer and whizz briefly, then add the remaining oil, the sherry vinegar and coriander. Whizz again until smooth and creamy. Check the seasoning, adding salt and pepper to taste. Pour into a bowl and keep warm; or reheat gently just before serving.

To serve, cut the meatloaf into thick slices and serve with some of the warm sauce.

# Chicken with pesto and tomato and basil sauce

**These chicken breasts are stuffed with pesto, breadcrumbs and Parmesan, then roasted until the skin is crispy and the meat tender. Instead of Parmesan and pesto, you could use a mixture of feta cheese and olive paste or goat's cheese and sun-dried tomato paste.**

Mix the breadcrumbs, pesto and Parmesan together, then season. Carefully ease the skin away from each chicken breast without detaching it from the meat: a little oil on your fingers helps. Then, using your fingers, push the stuffing under the skin. Replace the skin, patting gently, so that the pesto mixture is covered (don't worry if little bits poke out). Using a pastry brush, brush a little olive oil over the top of each breast and place on a lightly oiled baking tray. (The chicken can be prepared up to this stage 6 hours in advance and then refrigerated. Bring to room temperature 30 minutes before baking.)

Roast the chicken in an oven preheated to 220°C/425°F/Gas Mark 7 for 20–25 minutes or until it is just cooked. Test after 20 minutes by inserting the tip of a sharp knife into the thickest part of the flesh: the juices should run clear. Leave the chicken to rest for 5 minutes before serving.

For the sauce, heat the oil in a pan, add the garlic and fry gently for 2 minutes. Tip the oil and garlic into a food processor with the chopped tomatoes. Snip in the basil leaves and add the vinegar and stock. Whizz until it has a saucelike consistency. Season to taste with salt and pepper. (This can be prepared in advance, chilled, then reheated.) Heat the sauce gently until piping hot, then taste for seasoning.

Serve the chicken with the tomato sauce and a small spoonful of the pan juices.

## SERVES 4

4 tablespoons fresh brown breadcrumbs

2 tablespoons pesto

1 tablespoon freshly grated Parmesan cheese

4 large boneless free-range chicken breasts, unskinned

olive oil for brushing

salt and freshly ground black pepper

**For the tomato and basil sauce:**

2 tablespoons olive oil (preferably from the jar of tomatoes)

2 large garlic cloves, chopped

3 tablespoons sun-dried tomatoes, chopped

8 large fresh basil leaves

½ tablespoon balsamic vinegar

150ml/5fl oz chicken stock

# Slow-braised lamb shanks

You may have to order the shanks from your butcher. Follow this hearty, satisfying dish with a steamed pudding and you will have reached comfort-food nirvana.

Heat the oil in a large casserole and brown the shanks all over. If they are really large you might need to do this in 2 batches. Remove with a slotted spoon and add the garlic, onion and carrots to the pan. Fry gently for about 10 minutes, then stir in the tomatoes, rosemary, lamb stock and some salt and pepper. Bring to the boil, then return the meat to the pan. Season the meat and drizzle the honey over it. Cover tightly and cook in an oven preheated to 150°C/300°F/Gas Mark 2 for 3½–4 hours, until the meat is falling off the bone. Check the seasoning and serve with mashed potatoes and a green vegetable.

**SERVES 4**

| |
|---|
| 2 tablespoons olive oil |
| 4 large lamb shanks |
| 3 garlic cloves, chopped |
| 1 large onion, chopped |
| 450g/1lb large carrots, cut into large chunks |
| 400g tin of chopped tomatoes |
| 2 thick sprigs of fresh rosemary |
| 300ml/10fl oz lamb stock |
| 2 tablespoons runny honey |
| salt and freshly ground black pepper |

# Pork casserole with black pudding crust

Be sure your black pudding is the very best quality: in other words, buy it from a reputable butcher, preferably one who makes his own.
Serve with mashed potatoes and a green vegetable.

Heat the oil, half the butter and 2 teaspoons of the jelly in a casserole, add the pork and brown all over. Remove with a slotted spoon, then add the onion, leek and garlic and fry gently until softened. Return the meat to the casserole with the bay leaf, cider, stock, apple, pear and some salt and pepper. Bring to the boil, then cover and cook in an oven preheated to 170°C/325°F/Gas Mark 3 for about 40 minutes. Remove from the oven and increase the temperature to 180°C/350°F/Gas Mark 4.

With a deep ladle, remove about 150ml/5fl oz (2 ladlefuls) of the liquid and pour into a small saucepan. Add the remaining jelly and bring to the boil. Boil for 4–5 minutes or until reduced and thickened. Stir back into the casserole and adjust the seasoning to taste.

Dice the remaining butter. Place the black pudding slices on top of the casserole, overlapping them slightly, and dot with the diced butter. Bake, uncovered, in the oven for 25–30 minutes or until the top is crusty.

**SERVES 4**

| |
|---|
| 1 tablespoon olive oil |
| 25g/1oz butter |
| 3 teaspoons apple (or quince or redcurrant) jelly |
| 750g/1lb 10oz pork shoulder, trimmed and cut into chunks |
| 1 onion, chopped |
| 1 medium leek, finely sliced |
| 2 garlic cloves, chopped |
| 1 bay leaf |
| 150ml/5fl oz dry cider |
| 150ml/5fl oz chicken stock |
| 1 cooking apple, peeled, cored and diced |
| 1 pear, peeled, cored and diced |
| 175g/6oz black pudding, thinly sliced (skin removed if necessary) |
| salt and freshly ground black pepper |

# Luxury fish pie with prawns

## SERVES 6

1kg/2¼lb skinless white fish fillets, such as cod, haddock, coley or ling

450ml/16fl oz creamy milk

15g/½oz fresh parsley or dill (stalks and leaves), leaves chopped

8 peppercorns

50g/1¾oz butter

40g/1½oz plain flour

100ml/3½fl oz white wine

1 heaped tablespoon capers

grated zest of 1 small orange

350g/12oz cooked peeled tiger/king prawns

2 hard-boiled eggs, quartered

salt and freshly ground black pepper

### For the topping:

1.25kg/2¾lb potatoes, peeled and chopped

25g/1oz butter

200ml/7fl oz crème fraîche

freshly grated nutmeg

**If you intend to freeze this dish after assembling, be sure to use seafood that has not been previously frozen.**

For the topping, cook the potatoes in boiling salted water until soft, then drain thoroughly. Mash with 25g/1oz of the butter and the crème fraîche and season with plenty of salt and pepper and a tiny grating of nutmeg.

Place the fish fillets in a large saucepan with the milk, parsley or dill stalks (reserving the leaves for later) and peppercorns. Bring slowly to the boil, then reduce the heat, cover and simmer for 5 minutes. Strain the liquid into a jug. Break up the fish into large chunks and place in a large ovenproof dish. In another saucepan, melt the butter, then add the flour and cook for 1–2 minutes, stirring constantly. Remove from the heat and gradually add the reserved milk and the wine, whisking well. Return to the heat and cook for 8–10 minutes, whisking occasionally, until thickened. Remove from the heat and add the chopped parsley or dill leaves, capers, orange zest and plenty of salt and pepper.

Distribute the prawns and eggs on top of the fish and pour over the sauce, to cover. Spoon on the potatoes and gently smooth over. Fork up the top and allow to cool. (It can now be chilled overnight or frozen.)

Place in an oven preheated to 190°C/375°F/Gas Mark 5 for about 1 hour or until the centre is piping hot and the top golden brown. Cover with foil if it needs any longer to cook.

# Mussel and saffron crêpes

## SERVES 4

1kg/2¼lb mussels

150ml/5fl oz dry white wine

a pinch of saffron

25g/1oz butter

25g/1oz plain flour

100ml/3½fl oz double cream

grated zest of 1 small orange

1 tablespoon milk

salt and freshly ground black pepper

### For the crêpes:

75g/2¾oz plain flour

25g/1oz buckwheat flour

a pinch of salt

1 medium egg, beaten

300ml/10fl oz milk

**These crêpes are similar to galettes – pancakes made from buckwheat flour. Although it does add a wonderfully earthy, savoury taste to the crêpes, if you cannot buy buckwheat flour simply substitute plain flour.**

For the crêpes, place everything in a food processor and whizz until smooth (or whisk by hand). Transfer to a bowl, cover and chill for at least 1 hour.

Meanwhile, prepare the mussels. Scrub and de-beard them, discarding any with broken shells or any open ones that do not close when tapped on a work surface. Place the mussels in a heavy saucepan with the wine, bring to the boil, then cover and cook for about 4 minutes until the shells are open, shaking the pan occasionally. Strain though a sieve lined with a double layer of kitchen paper (to eliminate any grit). Save the liquid. Discard any unopened mussels, shell the rest and set aside. Add the saffron to the strained mussel liquor and leave for 10 minutes.

To make the crêpes, rub a hot crêpe pan with a little butter and pour in a tablespoon of batter. Swirl the batter around the pan and cook for 1–2 minutes, then flip over and cook for 1–2 minutes on the other side. Continue until you have 8–10 crêpes. Place 8 crêpes on a board (extras are cook's perks) and divide the mussels between them.

For the sauce, melt the butter in a saucepan, add the flour and stir to make a roux. Add the reserved saffron liquor and bring to the boil, whisking all the time. Reduce to a simmer, stir in the cream and orange zest and season to taste. Simmer for a couple of minutes.

Spoon about 2 tablespoons of the sauce over the mussels in each crêpe. Roll up and place in a buttered ovenproof dish. Thin down the remaining sauce (about 2 tablespoons) with the milk and drizzle over the crêpes. You can bake them immediately or cool and refrigerate the dish for up to 4 hours. Remove from the refrigerator 30 minutes before baking. Bake in an oven preheated to 180°C/350°F/Gas Mark 4 for about 20 minutes or until piping hot and bubbling.

When making lots of crêpes, don't bother to interleave them with greaseproof paper unless you intend to refrigerate or freeze them. If they have not stuck to the crêpe pan, they should not stick together.

# Shepherd's pie with parsnip topping

**Pedants among us demand that our shepherd's pie is made only of yesterday's roast lamb, minced up and covered with mashed potato. Cottage pie is the dish that uses minced beef. Quite so.**

**But, flying in the face of conformity, I give you my shepherd's pie – brazenly made with minced beef and topped with a mixture of parsnip, potato and soured cream. You can convert it into an 'American pie' (well, that is what it was called at my school dinners) by spreading a layer of baked beans between meat and potatoes. Oh, and a dish of peas is absolutely obligatory.**

Heat the oil in a large saucepan, add the onion and garlic and fry gently for about 10 minutes. Then increase the heat and add the mince. Brown it all over, stirring to break it up, for about 5 minutes. Sprinkle over the flour, stir, then add the hot stock. Bring to the boil and stir in the horseradish, tomato purée, Worcestershire sauce, parsley and some salt and pepper. Cover and cook for about 15 minutes.

Meanwhile, prepare the topping: cook the parsnips and potatoes in boiling salted water until tender, then drain well. Mash with the oil, butter, soured cream and nutmeg. Add plenty of salt and pepper to taste.

Tip the mince into a large shallow ovenproof dish, then top with the parsnip mixture. Fork up the top. Either cook the pie at once or leave to cool, then chill and cook later. (If it has been refrigerated, transfer to room temperature at least 30 minutes before heating.)

Cook in an oven preheated to 180°C/350°F/Gas Mark 4 for about 35–40 minutes or until the topping is golden brown and the meat piping hot.

## SERVES 6

| |
|---|
| 1 tablespoon olive oil |
| 1 large onion, finely chopped |
| 2 garlic cloves, chopped |
| 900g/2lb lean minced beef |
| 1 tablespoon plain flour |
| 300ml/10fl oz hot beef stock |
| 1 teaspoon horseradish sauce |
| 1 tablespoon tomato purée |
| 1 tablespoon Worcestershire sauce |
| 1 tablespoon chopped fresh parsley |
| salt and freshly ground black pepper |

**For the topping:**

| |
|---|
| 800g/1lb 12oz parsnips, peeled and chopped |
| 800g/1lb 12oz potatoes, peeled and chopped |
| 2 tablespoons olive oil |
| 25g/1oz butter |
| 150ml/5fl oz soured cream |
| a good grating of nutmeg |

# Lamb and tomato crêpe stack

## SERVES 4–6

1 teaspoon oil

500g/1lb 2oz lean minced lamb

2 teaspoons finely chopped fresh rosemary

4 heaped tablespoons sun-dried tomato purée

125g/4½oz Cos/romaine lettuce, shredded

1 tablespoon milk

65g/2½oz mature Cheddar cheese, grated

salt and freshly ground black pepper

**For the crêpes:**

125g/4½oz plain flour, sifted

a pinch of salt

1 medium egg

300ml/10fl oz milk

oil for frying

**For the sauce:**

50g/1¾oz butter

50g/1¾oz plain flour

450ml/16fl oz milk

a little grating of nutmeg

**This lovely recipe makes a stack of pancakes interspersed with lamb, sun-dried tomato purée, Cos lettuce and white sauce. Topped with lots of grated cheese, it is baked until golden and bubbling, then cut into wedges like a cake. Serve with a fresh tomato salad on the side.**

To make the crêpes, blend the flour, salt, egg and milk together in a food processor. Leave to stand for about half an hour if you have time. Lightly oil an 18–20cm/7–8in non-stick frying pan and make 5 crêpes, turning them when bubbles appear. Eat the rest (it makes 8–9) with lemon and sugar, to keep up your strength as you cook.

For the filling, heat the oil in a pan and fry the minced lamb gently until browned. Add the rosemary and half the tomato purée and and cook for about 15 minutes, uncovered, over a low heat. Season with salt and pepper, then drain over a sieve to eliminate any liquid.

For the sauce, melt the butter in a pan, stir in the flour and cook for 1 minute. Gradually whisk in the milk, then bring to the boil and simmer for about 5 minutes or until thick, whisking all the time. Season well with salt, pepper and nutmeg. Remove 2 tablespoons of the sauce and set aside. Mix the lettuce with the remaining hot sauce and check the seasoning.

Place 1 crêpe in a buttered shallow ovenproof dish about 23cm/9in in diameter. Spread it with ½ tablespoon of sun-dried tomato purée, then with half the lettuce mixture. Place another crêpe on top, spread with ½ tablespoon of tomato purée, then with half the lamb mixture. Repeat with the remaining tomato purée, sauce, lamb and 2 more crêpes.

Add the milk to the remaining white sauce in order to thin it down. Place the last crêpe on top of the pile, pour over the thinned-down sauce, sprinkle the cheese on top and bake in an oven preheated to 200°C/400°F/Gas Mark 6 for about 20 minutes, until golden brown on top and piping hot. (Alternatively, prepare a day in advance and chill. Bring to room temperature before baking on the day.) Cut into wedges to serve.

# Rabbit with green olives, figs and polenta

**SERVES 6**

| |
|---|
| 6 plump rabbit joints |
| 125g/4½oz dried figs, stems removed |
| 150g/5½oz large green olives, stoned |
| 65g/2½oz capers |
| 2 tablespoons sun-dried tomatoes |
| 3 large garlic cloves, finely chopped |
| 2 tablespoons chopped fresh oregano |
| 100ml/3½fl oz red wine vinegar |
| 1 tablespoon runny honey |
| 15g/½oz fresh flat-leaf parsley |
| 5–6 tablespoons olive oil, plus extra to serve |
| 200ml/7fl oz dry white wine |
| 350g/12oz instant polenta |
| 1.75 litres/3 pints water |
| salt and freshly ground black pepper |

**This is an Australian-inspired recipe, full of big, gutsy flavours. Match with a big, gutsy Ozzie red. If you buy olives and capers in brine, be sure to rinse and dry them thoroughly.**

Place the rabbit joints in a large, deep dish. Cut the figs, olives, capers and sun-dried tomatoes into thin slivers and place in a mixing bowl. Add the garlic, oregano, vinegar and honey. Remove the stalks from the parsley and chop them finely, reserving the leaves. Add the stalks to the bowl with 4 tablespoons of the olive oil and 4 tablespoons of the wine. Mix everything together, then pour the mixture over the rabbit and cover. Leave to marinate in a cool place for 4–8 hours.

Remove the rabbit from the marinade and pat dry. Season the rabbit and the marinade with salt and pepper. Heat the remaining oil in a heavy casserole and brown the rabbit all over (4–5 minutes). Add the marinade and the remaining wine, bring to the boil, then cover tightly and cook in an oven preheated to 170°C/325°F/Gas Mark 3 for 1½–2 hours, until the rabbit is tender and the sauce is thick. Finely chop the parsley leaves and stir them into the casserole. Taste and season with salt and pepper, then leave to cool slightly: it tastes better warm than hot.

Place the polenta in a large, heavy-based saucepan with the water and 2 teaspoons of salt. Bring slowly to the boil, stirring occasionally. Once bubbles appear, cook until thick, whisking constantly: 1–5 minutes, according to the packet instructions. Taste and season with salt and pepper, then stir in a good slug of olive oil.

To serve, place a mound of polenta on each warmed plate, then top with the rabbit and plenty of sauce.

# Fishcakes with salmon roe and soured cream

**These fishcakes can be frozen for up to two weeks, then cooked without defrosting. Instead of using cod and salmon, you could use smoked haddock and add either fresh crabmeat or shelled cockles.**

Place the cod and salmon in a saucepan with the milk and butter. Bring slowly to the boil, then, when bubbles appear on the surface, cover and cook for 3–4 minutes, until the fish is just done. Strain the fish in a sieve, reserving the liquid. Remove and discard the skin and any bones and flake the flesh into chunks.

Cook the potatoes in boiling salted water until tender, then drain thoroughly. Mash, then add the reserved fish-cooking liquid and continue mashing until smooth. Stir in 50g/1¾oz of the breadcrumbs with the herbs, lemon juice and horseradish. Season generously with salt and pepper and combine thoroughly, but not vigorously, with the fish: you want large chunks of fish intact. Form into 12 fishcakes: place a 7.5cm/3in pastry cutter or ring on a board and fill with some of the mixture, pressing well down. Slide a fish slice underneath and transfer to a flat plate, then carefully slip out the fish slice and lift off the cutter. Refrigerate for at least 2 hours.

Put the flour, beaten eggs and remaining breadcrumbs on 3 separate plates. Carefully coat the fishcakes with the flour, shaking off any excess, then the egg and finally the breadcrumbs. To freeze, place on a plate and 'open freeze' until solid – about 2 hours – then wrap and store in the freezer.

An hour before serving, remove the fishcakes from the freezer. Heat some oil in a frying pan and fry the still-frozen fishcakes for about 5 minutes, turning once, until golden brown all over. Drain briefly, then place on a baking tray in an oven preheated to 140°C/275°F/Gas Mark 1 for 45–55 minutes or until piping hot all the way through.

To serve, place 2 fishcakes on each warmed plate with a dollop each of salmon roe and soured cream.

## SERVES 6

400g/14oz cod fillet

400g/14oz salmon fillet

150ml/5fl oz milk

75g/2¾oz butter

700g/1lb 9oz potatoes (peeled weight)

200g/7oz fresh brown breadcrumbs

20g/¾oz fresh chives or parsley, chopped

1 tablespoon lemon juice

1 heaped teaspoon horseradish relish

2 tablespoons flour

2 large eggs, beaten

sunflower oil for frying

salt and freshly ground black pepper

salmon roe (keta) and soured cream, to serve

# Chicken with preserved lemons and black olives

This is based on a Moroccan dish made from preserved lemons. It is important to start thinking about it well in advance, as the lemons should be salted and preserved a couple of weeks beforehand to enhance the tangy lemon flavour. You must rinse the lemon slices really well, otherwise they will be too salty. Serve the chicken with couscous.

For the lemons, quarter each lemon and layer up in a Kilner jar, pressing 1 heaped teaspoon of salt over each lemon quarter as you layer. Sprinkle 2 tablespoons of salt over the lot, then pour over enough boiling water to cover. Leave until cold, then seal and leave somewhere cool for about 2 weeks.

For the chicken, heat the oil in heavy-based casserole, add the chicken pieces and fry for about 5 minutes, until browned all over (do this in 2 batches). Remove with a slotted spoon and add the onions to the casserole. Fry gently for about 10 minutes, then add the garlic, saffron and ginger. Fry for about 2 minutes, then return the chicken to the pan.

Rinse 4 lemon quarters well, then cut off and discard the pulp to leave only the peel. Cut the peel into slices and add these to the pan with the boiling water and some black pepper. Bring to the boil, cover and transfer to an oven preheated to 170°C/325°F/Gas Mark 3. Cook for about 30 minutes, then remove from the oven and stir in the olives. Cook for a further 20 minutes, then check the seasoning and serve.

## SERVES 4

2 tablespoons olive oil

8 free-range chicken pieces

2 onions, finely chopped

2 garlic cloves, chopped

1 level teaspoon saffron strands

½ teaspoon ground ginger

1 preserved lemon, cut into thick slices

200ml/7fl oz boiling water

24 black olives, stoned

salt and freshly ground black pepper

**For the preserved lemons:**

3 unwaxed lemons, washed

coarse sea salt

# Chicory and Gruyère tart

**SERVES 6**

4 heads of chicory, leaves separated

4 tablespoons olive oil

1 tablespoon semolina or polenta

150g/5½oz Gruyère cheese, grated

salt and freshly ground black pepper

**For the pastry:**

175g/6oz plain flour, sifted

75g/2¾oz medium oatmeal

½ teaspoon salt

150g/5½oz unsalted butter, diced

1 medium egg

1–1½ tablespoons olive oil

**This tart has wonderfully crunchy, oaty pastry and a gooey, cheesy filling.**

For the pastry, place the flour, oatmeal, salt and butter in a food processor and process until the mixture resembles breadcrumbs. Mix the egg with 1 tablespoon of the oil and pour in through the feeder tube as the machine is running. Add a little more oil if it needs it: it should have a dampish texture and come together easily in your hands. Wrap in clingfilm and chill for 1 hour. Roll out to fit a buttered deep, loose-bottomed 23cm/9in tart tin. Prick the base and chill for at least 2 hours, preferably overnight. Cover with foil and fill with baking beans, then bake blind at 190°C/375°F/Gas Mark 5 for 20 minutes. Remove the foil and bake for a further 10 minutes, until cooked through.

Arrange the chicory leaves in 2 layers in a large roasting tin, drizzling the oil over each layer and seasoning well. Cook in an oven preheated to 150°C/300°F/Gas Mark 2 for 45 minutes or until tinged with golden brown. Turn the leaves over half way through. Sprinkle the semolina or polenta over the pastry base, then top with the chicory. Sprinkle over the grated cheese and bake in an oven preheated to 180°C/350°F/Gas Mark 4 for 10–15 minutes or until the cheese is gloriously gooey and molten. Serve warm.

# Aubergine and mozzarella stack with salsa verde

**SERVES 4**

2 fat aubergines, each cut into
6 slices about 2cm/¾in thick

3–4 tablespoons olive oil

2 mozzarella cheeses, drained

salt and freshly ground black pepper

**For the salsa verde:**

25g/1oz fresh parsley

15g/½oz fresh mint

1 heaped tablespoon capers, drained

2 teaspoons Dijon mustard

2 garlic cloves, crushed

1 teaspoon white wine vinegar

4 tablespoons extra virgin olive oil

**This unbelievably tasty stack can be eaten either as a vegetarian main course, with a rocket salad, or as a substantial starter. Serve as soon as possible after assembling, otherwise everything will slide off.**

**I like to warm the cheese very slightly before adding it to this dish, to bring out the full flavour.**

For the salsa verde, place everything in a food processor and process until well blended. Season to taste with salt and pepper.

Sprinkle the aubergine slices with salt and leave for 30 minutes, then rinse and pat dry. Heat half the oil in a frying pan and fry half the aubergine slices for 3–4 minutes on each side, until golden brown. Add the remaining oil and fry the remaining aubergine. Cut each mozzarella into 4 slices and arrange in a dish. Place in an oven preheated to 110°C/225°F/Gas Mark ¼ for 4 minutes, until just warm but not yet beginning to melt.

To assemble, place an aubergine slice on each plate, top with a slice of cheese, then with a teaspoon of salsa. Repeat these layers once, then top with another aubergine slice and 2 teaspoons of salsa verde. Serve at once.

# Stuffed squid with lemon oil

Your fishmonger can prepare the squid for you, although it is an easy process (see page 12). If you cannot get one large squid (25–28cm/ 10–11in long, weighing about 500g/1lb 2oz including the tentacles), use two smaller ones and reduce the cooking time to 1 hour. You can cook this in advance and leave, covered with the foil, for up to an hour. It is best served barely warm, not hot.

If you cannot find commercial lemon oil, then infuse some pared lemon rind in extra virgin olive oil for a few days, strain and use.

Remove the tentacles of the squid and reserve them for another use, such as a stir-fry. Now all you should have is the cleaned body section.

Mix together the cockles, breadcrumbs, egg, lemon zest and juice and pesto and season well. Stuff the squid with the filling, packing it well down. Make sure the filling is not bulging out of the hole or the squid will burst. Secure the opening with 2 cocktail sticks and place the squid in an ovenproof dish. Pour over the sherry, cover tightly with oiled foil and cook in an oven preheated to 170°C/325°F/Gas Mark 3 for 1¼ hours or until the squid feels tender when gently prodded with a fork. Remove from the oven and leave to rest for at least 15 minutes. Serve cut into slices, drizzled with lemon oil.

## SERVES 6

| |
|---|
| 1 large prepared squid |
| 150g/5½oz cooked cockles (or small prawns) |
| 200g/7oz fresh wholemeal breadcrumbs |
| 1 medium egg |
| grated zest and juice of 1 lemon |
| 1 heaped tablespoon pesto |
| 3 tablespoons dry (fino) sherry |
| salt and freshly ground black pepper |
| lemon oil, to serve |

# Herb and mustard roast chicken

The chicken is flavoured with a herb and mustard dressing, inserted between the skin and flesh to keep it really moist. It ends up beautifully succulent and needs no gravy, as the pan juices are extremely tasty.

Place the chicken in a roasting tin. Season the inside with salt and pepper and place the onion and lemon quarters in the cavity.

Put the mustard, vinegar, oil and herbs in a screw-top jar and shake until amalgamated, then season. Slide your fingers between the chicken skin and breast meat, down the backbone, to form a pocket. Gently ease about half the dressing under the skin. Using a teaspoon and your fingers, spread it over the breast meat. Pour the remaining dressing over the chicken. Roast in an oven preheated to 200°C/400°F/Gas Mark 6 for 20 minutes, then reduce the temperature to 180°C/350°F/Gas Mark 4 and cook for a further 20 minutes per 450g/1lb, basting every 20 minutes. It is cooked if the juices run clear when a sharp knife is inserted in the leg. Remove from the oven and leave to rest for 20 minutes, then carve and serve with the pan juices poured over.

## SERVES 4

| |
|---|
| 1 x 1.4–1.5kg/3lb 3oz–3lb 5oz free-range chicken |
| ½ onion, quartered |
| ½ lemon, quartered |
| 1 level tablespoon Dijon mustard |
| 2 teaspoons white wine vinegar |
| 4 tablespoons extra virgin olive oil |
| 2 heaped tablespoons chopped mixed fresh herbs (such as chervil, parsley, tarragon and sage) |
| salt and freshly ground black pepper |

**P**arties and dinners are memorable not only because of the food but also because of the anticipation of the event, the fine napery, the candles, flowers and gleaming glasses. There is more emphasis on sophisticated food, depending on whether it is a family event, such as Christmas or Easter, or a specifically adult 'do' such as Burns Night or a cocktail party. I find that when children are involved in any grand lunch or dinner it is not worth preparing anything too elaborate. Sadly, British children's palates, on the whole, are not as refined at such an early age as, say, French children's. I always remember marvelling at a French friend's toddlers tucking in to olives, artichokes and oysters with equanimity. My children recoil in horror when there is even one mushroom lurking in the depths of a stew.

However, I do think it is important to introduce children to an interesting variety of foods as early as possible, with the hope that gradually their palates will develop. If we feed them fish fingers and chips until they leave school there is little chance that they will suddenly become sophisticated gourmets the minute they enter adulthood. Regular family meals eaten together will surely equip children with the social skills required for special occasions. Hopefully they will begin to appreciate that food is not there simply to fill a gap; it is one of life's most sensual pleasures.

# CHAPTER NINE
# dinners and parties

**MAKES 24**

| |
|---|
| 3 large sheets of filo pastry (about 45 x 25cm/18 x 10in) |
| 25g/1oz unsalted butter, melted |
| 1 tablespoon olive oil |
| 150ml/5fl oz double cream |
| ½ teaspoon saffron strands (a generous pinch) |
| 2 medium egg yolks |
| 65–75g/2½–2¾oz mature manchego cheese, grated |
| salt and freshly ground black pepper |

**These are ideal to serve as canapés with drinks. Bake them in advance and just reheat briefly before serving. If you cannot find manchego (a Spanish ewe's milk cheese), use a mixture of mature Cheddar and Parmesan.**

Lay out the sheets of filo pastry on a work surface. Working quickly so the filo does not dry out, mix together the melted butter and the oil. Using a pastry brush, brush all over a sheet of filo. Place a second sheet on top, brush all over, then top with the third sheet. Brush all over again with the butter mixture.

Lightly grease 2 mini-muffin pans – to make 24 tartlets altogether. Cut the filo layers into 24 squares. Line each mini-muffin cup with a filo square, pressing in lightly. Do not worry about ragged edges. Chill for at least 30 minutes, then bake in an oven preheated to 190°C/375°F/Gas Mark 5 for 10 minutes, until crisp and lightly browned. Leave to cool.

For the filling, bring the cream to the boil in a small pan. Once bubbling, stir in the saffron, then remove from the heat, cover and leave to infuse for about 30 minutes. Whisk in the egg yolks and plenty of salt and pepper.

Fill each tartlet with about half the grated cheese. Carefully pour the saffron custard over each one and top with the remaining cheese. Bake for 8–10 minutes, until the filling sets. Serve warm.

## A cocktail party

| | |
|---|---|
| **Thai fish balls with dipping sauce** | 73 |
| **Spicy chicken kebabs** | 108 |
| **Saffron and manchego tartlets** | |
| **Cheese-stuffed rice balls** | 138 |

## Joanna's wine notes

Dry sparkling whites, including Champagne, work well with these spicy canapés. Australia, New Zealand, California and South Africa all make good sparkling wine, while Cava from Spain is a cheaper option. But fizz isn't essential. Many still, dry whites are suitable, e.g. from Alsace, or north Italians such as Lugana and Bianco di Custoza.

**Cheese-stuffed rice balls (page 138), Saffron and manchego tartlets**

# Parmesan snaps

**MAKES 6**

100g/3½oz block of Parmesan cheese (this is the weight without rind, so buy a larger piece)

a little oil

**So called because they are rather like brandy snaps but savoury. In fact the ingredients for the snaps are nothing but grated Parmesan cheese, pure and simple. They form lovely, light, lacy cracknels.**

**It is important to grate the cheese freshly for this recipe; prepacked grated Parmesan will not do as it will undoubtedly be too finely grated. Serve the snaps with drinks. Or mould them into baskets (as you would for brandy snap baskets, by draping them over an orange while still warm) and fill with a light salad for a sophisticated starter or lunch.**

Grate the Parmesan coarsely; I use the grating blade on my food processor. Lightly oil a baking sheet, then drop the cheese on to it in 6 piles. Spread it out to form circles about 10cm/4in in diameter. Bake in an oven preheated to 200°C/400°F/Gas Mark 6 for about 5 minutes, until bubbling and lacy-looking. Remove and leave for a few seconds. Then loosen around the edges with a spatula and carefully transfer to a wire rack (or mould over an orange if you want a basket shape). Leave to cool; they will crisp up as they cool. Serve cold.

# Cheese-stuffed rice balls

**MAKES ABOUT 24**

25g/1oz butter

1 tablespoon olive oil

1 onion, finely chopped

250g/9oz risotto rice

900ml/1½ pints hot chicken stock

75g/2¾oz fresh breadcrumbs

1 medium egg, beaten

75g/2¾oz Parmesan cheese, freshly grated

2 tablespoons chopped fresh parsley or basil

100g/3½oz mozzarella cheese, cut into small cubes

vegetable oil for deep-frying

salt and freshly ground black pepper

**These deep-fried little balls of risotto are based on the Italian *arancini* and make an ideal canapé – or a starter if served with a little salad.**

To make the risotto, heat the butter and oil in a pan, add the onion and cook for 2 minutes. Add the rice and cook for another 2 minutes, stirring to coat the rice with the fat. Gradually stir in the stock, a little at a time, until all the liquid is absorbed and the rice is tender – about 20 minutes. Season to taste and leave to cool.

Toast the breadcrumbs in an oven preheated to 170°C/325°F/Gas Mark 3 until dried – about 30 minutes. Mix the egg, Parmesan and herbs into the risotto mixture. With dampened hands, shape the mixture into walnut-sized balls, then push a cube or two of mozzarella into the centre of each one, making sure the cheese is completely covered by the rice. Roll the balls in the breadcrumbs to coat and then chill for a couple of hours.

Heat plenty of oil in a deep-fryer to 180°C/350°F, or heat it in a deep, heavy-based pan and test the temperature by dropping in a small cube of bread; it should brown in 1½ minutes. Deep-fry the balls in batches for about 5–6 minutes, until crisp and golden brown. Drain on kitchen paper before serving. (They can be made in advance and reheated in a low oven.)

# Pheasants breasts with mango sauce

**If you cannot buy pheasant breasts, cut them from the birds yourself by running a sharp knife as close to the backbone as possible. Simmer the carcasses with parsley stalks and thyme to make stock or soup.**
**Serve the pheasant breasts with some braised celery and rice.**

Rub the pheasant breasts with a little olive oil, then cover and refrigerate for a couple of hours.

Purée the mango flesh with the lime juice in a food processor, then mix with the crème fraîche and mango chutney. Pour into a saucepan. (This can be kept, covered, in the refrigerator for a couple of hours.)

Heat the oil in a frying pan and brown the pheasant breasts all over, then season lightly and transfer them to an oiled baking sheet. Place in an oven preheated to 220°C/425°F/Gas Mark 7 for about 8 minutes, until just cooked.

Bring the sauce to the boil, simmer for a couple of minutes, then taste for seasoning and serve with the pheasant breasts.

## SERVES 6

6 pheasant breasts, skinned

1 large ripe mango, peeled and diced

juice of ½ lime

250ml/9fl oz crème fraîche

3 tablespoons mango chutney

2 tablespoons olive oil, plus extra for rubbing over the pheasant

salt and freshly ground black pepper

# Pheasant with gin

**Be sure to use young pheasant for this quick-roast recipe; older birds are better consigned to the casserole pot. Ask your butcher or game dealer for advice about age.**

Heat the butter in a frying pan, then add the juniper berries. Once hot, add the pheasant and brown them all over – about 5 minutes. Transfer to a roasting tin and pour over the butter from the pan. Season with salt and pepper. Place in an oven preheated to 200°C/400°F/Gas Mark 6 for 40–50 minutes, depending on size. Baste well every 10–15 minutes. Transfer to a board, cover with foil and leave to rest for 10–15 minutes, before carving into thin slices.

Meanwhile, spoon off most of the fat from the roasting tin, leaving about 1 tablespoon. Set the tin directly on the stove over a medium heat. Pour in the gin (carefully if you are using gas – it might ignite), then stir well to scrape up all the caramelized bits. Let it bubble away for about 5 minutes, until reduced by half, then lower the heat and add the redcurrant jelly. Stir until dissolved, then stir in the crème fraîche. Increase the heat again and bubble for 2–3 minutes. Season to taste, strain into a jug and serve with the pheasant.

## SERVES 6

75g/2¾oz butter

5–6 juniper berries, crushed

2 medium or large pheasant

150ml/5fl oz gin

2 tablespoons redcurrant jelly

200ml/7fl oz crème fraîche

salt and freshly ground black pepper

# Roast grouse with blackcurrants

**SERVES 2**

2 young grouse

50g/1¾oz butter, softened

75g/2¾oz blackcurrants

6 streaky bacon rashers

150ml/5fl oz red wine

2 teaspoons blackcurrant jelly

salt and freshly ground black pepper

**When in season, a roast grouse is a real treat. It is always a good idea to wait until later in the season (it opens, of course, on the Glorious Twelfth of August), when prices have come down and the birds are slightly larger. But they never become terribly large and so you should count on one per person. Serve this with fried breadcrumbs (or skirlie – a Scottish fried oatmeal dish) and a green vegetable. A wee dram (before or after) is also a very good idea.**

Wash and dry the insides of the grouse thoroughly. Mix together the softened butter and blackcurrants, trying not to squash the blackcurrants. Season with salt and pepper. Spoon half this mixture into each bird. Cover the top of each grouse with 3 rashers of bacon, then place them in a small, buttered heatproof dish or roasting tin. Pour over the red wine and roast in an oven preheated to 220°C/425°F/Gas Mark 7 for about 15–20 minutes, depending on size.

Transfer the birds to a carving board, cover with foil and leave to rest for about 10 minutes. Meanwhile, place the dish in which they were cooked over a direct heat and bubble until the liquid is reduced by half. Add the blackcurrant jelly and stir well. Season to taste with salt and pepper and serve with the grouse, on warmed plates.

# Duck with orange-roasted radicchio

**SERVES 8**

8 large duck breasts

3 large radicchio heads

4 tablespoons olive oil

3 tablespoons freshly squeezed orange juice

salt and freshly ground black pepper

**Serve this with sauté potatoes, cooked in the duck fat.**

Score the skin of each duck breast with a sharp knife. Heat a heavy-based frying pan until very hot, then place 4 duck breasts in it, skin-side down (with no added fat). Cook for 2 minutes, then season with salt and pepper and turn. Cook for a further minute, then season again and remove from the pan. Cook the remaining breasts in the same way. Place in an ovenproof dish and roast in an oven preheated to 220°C/425°F/Gas Mark 7 for 12–15 minutes. Meanwhile, remove the outer leaves of the radicchio (save the smaller leaves for a salad) and place these in a roasting tin – about 20 large leaves. Season, then drizzle over the olive oil and orange juice.

Once the duck is done, transfer it to a carving board, cover with foil and leave to rest for 10 minutes. Roast the radicchio in the oven for 8–10 minutes, until slightly wilted.

To serve, place a couple of radicchio leaves on each warm serving plate, slice the duck breasts and place on top. Spoon over the radicchio pan juices.

# Juniper gratin

This creamy, juniper-flavoured gratin can be made with potatoes and parsnips or just potatoes. It is the ideal accompaniment to any roast game or pork dish.

Place the potatoes and parsnips in a heavy-based saucepan with the cream, milk, salt and crushed juniper berries. Bring slowly to the boil, then simmer gently for 2 minutes, stirring carefully so the slices do not break up.

Season lightly with pepper. Tip into a buttered shallow gratin dish. Dot with butter and bake in an oven preheated to 180°C/350°F/Gas Mark 4 for about 1–1¼ hours or until golden brown, crusty and tender. Leave to stand for about 10 minutes before serving.

## SERVES 6

500g/1lb 2oz large potatoes, peeled and thinly sliced

500g/1lb 2oz parsnips, peeled and thinly sliced

300ml/10fl oz double cream

100ml/3½fl oz milk

2 teaspoons salt

20–24 juniper berries, crushed

a little butter for dotting

freshly ground black pepper

# Saffron mash

This makes a good accompaniment to grilled or roast cod, seafood stews or roast pork.

In a small saucepan, gently heat the milk, cream, butter and saffron. Once the butter has melted, remove from the heat, cover and leave to stand for at least 20 minutes. Meanwhile, boil the potatoes in salted water until tender, then drain well until completely dry. Using a potato masher, mash the potatoes well, then add the saffron mixture. Mash well again, adding salt and pepper to taste. Serve piping hot.

## SERVES 6–8

125ml/4fl oz milk

125ml/4fl oz double cream

100g/3½oz butter

½ teaspoon saffron strands (a generous pinch)

1kg/2¼lb potatoes, peeled and cut into chunks

salt and freshly ground black pepper

# Roast monkfish with garlic, rosemary and bacon

## SERVES 4

1 monkfish tail (about 900g/2lb)

1 large sprig of fresh rosemary

2 garlic cloves, peeled and cut into thin slivers

6 streaky bacon rashers

150ml/5fl oz red wine

1 tablespoon olive oil

salt and freshly ground black pepper

**When you are inserting the garlic and rosemary in the monkfish tail, try to make incisions directly opposite each other over the bone, so that when you wrap the bacon around the fish it can go between the incisions.**

Place the fish in a roasting tin. Pull off smaller sprigs of rosemary. Make 8–10 small incisions in the fish on either side of the bone. Push a garlic sliver and rosemary sprig into each. Season the fish well with salt and pepper, then wrap bacon rashers around it, in between the incisions. Pour over the red wine and drizzle over the oil.

Roast in an oven preheated to 220°C/425°F/Gas Mark 7 for 30 minutes, basting twice, then remove the fish from the oven and leave to rest for at least 5 minutes.

Carve into slices and serve with the pan juices and sauté potatoes.

# Salt- and dill-cured salmon

## SERVES 8

1kg/2¼lb boneless salmon fillet, skin on

3 teaspoons sugar

4 teaspoons sea salt

4 tablespoons chopped fresh dill

ground white pepper

### For the sauce:

2 tablespoons Dijon mustard

1 tablespoon white wine vinegar

2 tablespoons vegetable oil

a pinch each of sugar, salt and pepper

**Similar to the Swedish *gravadlax* – literally 'buried salmon' – this Finnish recipe is not buried (i.e. weighted down) and is less sweet. All over Scandinavia, cured salmon is served as a main course with boiled new potatoes. For a starter, I suggest serving the salmon slices with dark rye bread and a simple mustard sauce. Any leftover salmon is wonderful with fresh bagels and cream cheese for breakfast.**

Place the fish on a large piece of baking parchment, skin-side down. Mix the sugar, salt and dill with plenty of white pepper and rub this mixture over the surface of the fish. Wrap in the baking parchment, place in a dish and then in the refrigerator for 24 hours.

To make the sauce, mix the mustard and vinegar together, then slowly whisk in the remaining ingredients.

Carefully unwrap the fish and drain off the liquid. Pat dry gently with kitchen paper, then cut diagonally into thin slices and serve with the mustard sauce and some rye bread.

# Salmon fillets with stir-fried cabbage and roasted garlic aïoli

**Ask your fishmonger to remove the pin bones from the skinned salmon fillets, or do it yourself by running your fingers over them and removing the tiny bones with tweezers.**

First roast the garlic for the aïoli. Place the cloves in a small ovenproof dish with a teaspoon of olive oil and cook in an oven preheated to 180°C/350°F/ Gas Mark 4 for 20–25 minutes, until tender. Once cool, snip off the end of each clove and squeeze the soft insides into a food processor. Add the mustard, egg and salt. Process for 20–30 seconds, then add the lemon juice and process for a few seconds longer. With the machine running, very slowly pour in first the sunflower oil and then sufficient olive oil to achieve the consistency of a thinnish mayonnaise. Season well with salt, pepper and lemon juice.

Remove the salmon from the refrigerator 30 minutes before cooking. Place on an oiled baking tray, lightly brush with olive oil and sprinkle with sea salt. Cook in the centre of an oven preheated to 240°C/475°F/Gas Mark 9 for 7–8 minutes, then remove from the oven and leave to rest for 3–4 minutes.

Heat the sunflower oil in a wok or large frying pan. Once it is very hot, add the fish sauce and stand back; it will splutter. Immediately add the garlic, stir around, then add the cabbage and stir-fry for about 5 minutes, until it is just cooked but still crunchy. Add 1 teaspoon of sesame oil, then taste and add salt and pepper, plus more sesame oil if necessary.

To serve, place a small mound of cabbage on each warm plate. Top with a salmon fillet and spoon over the aïoli.

If you buy salmon fillets with the skin on, do not throw away the skin: brush it with oil, grill for 3–4 minutes until crispy, then snip it over a salad.

## SERVES 4

4 middle-cut salmon fillets (about 200g/7oz each), skinned and pin bones removed

olive oil for brushing

1½ tablespoons sunflower oil

1½ tablespoons Thai fish sauce (*nam pla*)

1 garlic clove, crushed

400g/14oz white cabbage, shredded

1–2 teaspoons sesame oil

sea salt and freshly ground black pepper

**For the aïoli:**

3 large garlic cloves, unpeeled

about 125ml/4fl oz olive oil

¼ teaspoon Dijon mustard

1 medium free-range egg

a pinch of salt

1 tablespoon lemon juice

75ml/3fl oz sunflower oil

| A spring lunch | | Joanna's wine notes |
|---|---|---|
| Asparagus with soft-boiled eggs | 77 | |
| Salmon fillets with stir-fried cabbage and roasted garlic aïoli | | |
| Warm rhubarb compote with white chocolate sorbet | 171 | |

### Joanna's wine notes

Sauvignon Blanc is good with asparagus but Chardonnay is better with eggs. The solution is Chablis, made from the Chardonnay grape, but with Sauvignon's crispness. It will go with the salmon too, but so will richer Chardonnays (e.g. California or Burgundy) and Pinot Noir reds. For a red to drink with both asparagus and salmon, try a Loire (e.g. Chinon or Saumur-Champigny).

# Roast pork with cinnamon apples

**SERVES 8**

1.5kg/3lb 5oz boned loin of outdoor-reared pork, with skin intact

olive oil

3 large Cox's (or Braeburn) apples

50g/1¾oz unsalted butter, softened

2 teaspoons ground cinnamon

350ml/12fl oz dry cider

2–3 tablespoons double cream

salt and freshly ground black pepper

**There is no mystery about making good crackling: simply allow the skin to dry out completely (store the joint unwrapped in the refrigerator), then salt the scored skin well and roast in a hot oven. Do not baste while cooking, as you would with other joints.**

**Serve this with Saffron Mash (see page 141) and a green vegetable.**

Either ask your butcher to score the rind of the pork or do it yourself, using a very sharp knife to score through the skin but not right through the fat. An hour or so before cooking, rub salt all over the skin and leave at room temperature. Just before cooking, wipe off the salt, then rub lightly with olive oil. Sprinkle over some more salt and rub it into the scored lines. Roast in an oven preheated to 220°C/425°F/Gas Mark 7 for 30 minutes, then reduce the temperature to 190°C/375°F/Gas Mark 5 and continue to cook for 1 hour per 1kg/2¼lb.

Meanwhile, prepare the apples: peel and core them, then cut each one into 6 wedges. Beat together the softened butter and cinnamon. Heat this mixture in a frying pan and, once hot, add the apples. Cook for 1 minute, then add 200ml/7fl oz of the cider and cook, uncovered, for about 20 minutes, until the apples are tender and the liquid reduced to just enough to coat the apples.

Once the pork is cooked, transfer to a board and leave to rest for 10 minutes. Pour away most of the fat in the roasting tin, leaving 1–1½ tablespoons. Add the remaining cider and bubble away for a few minutes, scraping up all the caramelized bits from the base of the tin. Stir in the cream and some salt and pepper to taste. Carve the pork and serve with the apples and gravy.

| A family sunday lunch | | Joanna's wine notes |
|---|---|---|
| **Roast pork with cinnamon apples** | | Pork accommodates both red and white wine but the creamy cinnamon apples are better served by white. The fruity sweetness of a medium-dry still Vouvray or German Riesling Spätlese is ideal; a ripe Chardonnay (e.g. from Chile or Australia) would also cope well. |
| **Saffron mash** | 141 | |
| **Mexican bread and butter pudding** | 174 | With the pudding: a sticky sweet Muscat de Beaumes de Venise or Australian Liqueur Muscat. |
| **Warm date cake with coconut fudge topping** | 188 | |

**Roast pork with cinnamon apples and Saffron mash**

# Roast cod with a coconut and lime sauce and mango salsa

## SERVES 4

4 thick pieces of cod fillet, skinned

2 tablespoons olive oil

salt and freshly ground black pepper

sprigs of fresh coriander, to serve

**For the mango salsa:**

2 large ripe mangoes, peeled, stoned and chopped

½ small red onion, finely chopped

1 tablespoon Thai fish sauce (*nam pla*)

1 teaspoon soy sauce

½ red chilli, deseeded and finely chopped

2 tablespoons chopped fresh coriander

1 tablespoon freshly squeezed lime juice

**For the coconut and lime sauce:**

2 tablespoons rice vinegar

2 teaspoons freshly grated root ginger

100g/3½oz creamed coconut (half a block)

3 tablespoons freshly squeezed lime juice

1 tablespoon Thai fish sauce (*nam pla*)

2 tablespoons coconut milk (from a can)

3 tablespoons finely chopped fresh coriander

**Add more chilli to the salsa if you prefer it really hot – taste as you go. Serve this with a green salad and some wild rice.**

Place the cod on a lightly oiled baking tray and drizzle over the olive oil. Using your fingers, rub it gently over the surface of the fish. Set aside to come to room temperature for an hour or so.

For the salsa, combine everything in a bowl, then add some freshly ground pepper. Taste and adjust the seasoning: it should not need any salt as the fish and soy sauces are salty. Stir well and leave to stand for about 1 hour.

For the sauce, combine everything except the coriander in a saucepan. Place over a gentle heat until the creamed coconut melts, then simmer very gently for about 4–5 minutes. Just before serving, add the coriander, taste and season with pepper if necessary.

Season the fish with salt and pepper and place in an oven preheated to 230°C/450°F/Gas Mark 8 for 8–10 minutes, until just cooked. To serve, place a mound of mango salsa on each plate, top with the cod and spoon some of the coconut and lime sauce all around the plate. Garnish each serving plate with a sprig or two of coriander.

# Chicken and mushroom lasagne

**This recipe can be frozen completely before baking. If you prefer to cook it straight away, then just cook for 10 minutes or so less than the time given below.**

**Instead of cooking the chicken from scratch you could use leftover chicken: you will need about 900g/2lb.**

**Serve with a tossed green salad.**

Place the chicken breasts in a large saucepan and add flavourings such as peppercorns or bay leaves. Cover with water and bring to the boil, then cover the pan and simmer for about 15–20 minutes, until the chicken is just cooked. Remove the chicken from the pan and leave to cool.

Meanwhile, heat 1 tablespoon of the olive oil in a saucepan and add the onion and half the garlic. Fry gently for 5 minutes, then add the tomatoes and their juices and 2 sprigs of the parsley. Bring to the boil, stirring, then simmer, uncovered, for about 20 minutes. Tip into a liquidizer and whizz until blended. Season well.

Finely chop the remaining parsley. Heat the remaining oil in another saucepan and fry the remaining garlic for 1 minute, then add the mushrooms. Cook gently for about 5 minutes, then stir in 2 tablespoons of the cream. Increase the heat and cook, uncovered, until the liquid has reduced enough to coat the mushrooms. Season and add the chopped parsley.

Once the chicken is cool enough to handle, break the flesh into large pieces and add it to the mushrooms. Whisk together the mascarpone, eggs, remaining cream and Parmesan. Season well.

To assemble, lightly oil a large lasagne dish, then tip in half the tomato sauce. Cover with a third of the lasagne sheets. Spoon over half the chicken and mushrooms. Top with half the mascarpone mixture, then another layer of lasagne. Top with the remaining tomato sauce, then the remaining chicken and mushrooms. Top with a third layer of lasagne and the remaining mascarpone mixture, smoothing over the top. Leave until completely cold, then place, uncovered, in the freezer. Overwrap in clingfilm once solid.

To cook, remove from the freezer and leave at room temperature for an hour or so. Remove the clingfilm and cover loosely with oiled foil. Bake in an oven preheated to 190°C/375°F/Gas Mark 5 for 35 minutes, then remove the foil and cook for a further 30 minutes or until piping hot. Leave to rest for about 15 minutes, then serve.

## SERVES 6

6 corn-fed or free-range chicken breasts

a few peppercorns and/or bay leaves

3 tablespoons olive oil

1 onion, chopped

4 garlic cloves, chopped

2 x 400g tins of tomatoes

15g/½oz fresh flat-leaf parsley

500g/1lb 2oz mushrooms, chopped

300ml/10fl oz double cream

250g/9oz mascarpone cheese

2 medium eggs

65g/2½oz Parmesan cheese, freshly grated

250g/9oz pre-cooked lasagne sheets

salt and freshly ground black pepper

# Chinese noodle salad with mango, crab and ginger

This is ideal for a buffet table, as it can be made up to six hours in advance, kept in the refrigerator and simply tossed well before serving.

For the dressing, shake everything together in a screw-top jar. Taste and add extra Tabasco if you want it hotter.

Cook the noodles according to the packet instructions, then drain well and toss them in the dressing while still warm. Leave to cool, then add the crab, spring onions, coriander, mangoes and papaya, tossing gently to mix evenly. (At this stage the salad can be covered and chilled for 6 hours.)

Just before serving, toss again and pile in a mound on a serving plate, garnished with the tiger prawns and with toasted sesame seeds and fresh coriander leaves, if liked.

## SERVES 8

2 x 250g packets of dried egg noodles

500g/1lb 2oz white crabmeat

6 large spring onions, chopped

3 heaped tablespoons chopped fresh coriander

2 large ripe mangoes, peeled, stoned and diced

1 large ripe papaya, peeled, deseeded and diced

250g/9oz cooked tiger prawns

toasted sesame seeds and fresh coriander leaves, to garnish (optional)

### For the dressing:

1 heaped tablespoon freshly grated root ginger

150ml/5fl oz sunflower oil

2 tablespoons freshly squeezed lime juice

1 tablespoon Thai fish sauce (*nam pla*)

several shakes of Tabasco (or hot chilli sauce)

salt and freshly ground black pepper

## Boxing day buffet (8-10)

| | |
|---|---|
| **Turkey tonnato** | 151 |
| **Chinese noodle salad with mango, crab and ginger** | |
| **Mint couscous tabbouleh** | 49 |
| **Layered chocolate and cranberry cream** | 170 |

## Joanna's wine notes

After the excesses of the day before, we all need something bright and reviving to drink. A fresh, not too oaky white, such as an Hungarian Chardonnay, a white Mâcon-Villages or a north Italian Lugana, would go with all the savoury dishes. For the Chinese noodles on their own, try an exotic, spicy Viognier or an Alsace Gewürztraminer.

# Tarragon turkey

1 x 3kg/6½lb free-range turkey

75g/2¾oz butter, softened

15g/½oz fresh tarragon, chopped

2 heaped tablespoons plain flour

250ml/9fl oz Noilly Prat (or white wine)

750ml/1¼ pints hot chicken (or turkey giblet) stock

salt and freshly ground black pepper

**For the stuffing:**

15g/½oz fresh tarragon

zest and juice of 1 large lemon

100g/3½oz pecan nuts

50g/1¾oz fresh breadcrumbs

2 medium eggs

**This is suitable for either Christmas or Thanksgiving and, unusually (certainly in my household), is enjoyed by both adults and fussy children!**

To make the stuffing, put the tarragon, lemon zest and juice, pecans and breadcrumbs in a food processor. Whizz briefly, then mix in the eggs and some salt and pepper.

Place the turkey in a large roasting tin. Push half the stuffing into the neck end (don't pack it in too tightly) and the other half into the body cavity, flattening it down well. Beat together the softened butter and chopped tarragon. Rub this all over the bird, then season with salt and pepper. Roast in an oven preheated to 220°C/425°F/Gas Mark 7 for 20 minutes. Turn the heat down to 190°C/375°F/Gas Mark 5 and cook for a further 1¼ hours, basting every 20–30 minutes, or until the bird is cooked through: begin testing after 1¼ hours by inserting a skewer or a sharp knife into the thickest part of the flesh; the juices should run clear. Once it is cooked, transfer the bird to a carving board and loosely cover with foil. Leave to rest for at least 15 minutes.

Spoon off excess fat from the roasting tin, leaving about 2 tablespoons. Place the tin over direct heat and add the flour. Stir well, scraping up all the bits from the base of the tin, then slowly pour in the Noilly Prat and stock. Whisking constantly, cook over a medium heat for 8–10 minutes until smooth. Taste for seasoning and serve with the sliced turkey and stuffing.

# Pumpkin wedges

1 small or ½ large pumpkin, wiped clean

3 tablespoons olive oil

salt and freshly ground black pepper

**Although you can peel the pumpkin before cooking, I find the flesh stays intact if you keep the peel on. Serve this as a side dish to Tarragon Turkey (see above) or on its own, perhaps topped with a little grated Parmesan and some pesto for a vegetarian dish.**

Cut the pumpkin into large wedges and remove and discard the fibres and seeds. Place the wedges on a baking tray and drizzle with the olive oil. Season with salt and pepper. Bake in an oven preheated to 200°C/400°F/Gas Mark 6 for 45–50 minutes or until tender.

# Turkey tonnato

The classic *tonnato* of northern Italy is usually prepared with veal but the sauce – a tuna mayonnaise – also works beautifully with cold turkey. And on Boxing Day, when the glorious roast bird, star of the previous day's feast, lingers threateningly in the larder, it provides yet another idea for using up all that leftover meat.

Lay the sliced turkey on a serving plate. Place the mayonnaise, tuna and half the anchovies in a food processor with the wine. Process until well combined, then taste and add salt and pepper if required. You might also want to add a little lemon juice.

Spoon the tuna mayonnaise over the turkey. Cut the remaining anchovies in half lengthways. Place these in a criss-cross pattern on top of the tuna sauce. Dot each square with a couple of capers or caper berries. Serve at room temperature.

## SERVES 8

leftover turkey meat, sliced

400g jar of good-quality mayonnaise

2 x 200g tins of tuna, drained

50g tin of anchovies, drained

4 tablespoons dry white wine

lemon juice (optional)

salt and freshly ground black pepper

capers or caper berries, to garnish

# Partridge with wild mushroom sauce

This makes the perfect supper for two for a special occasion. If you do have truffle oil (preferably white) to hand, it will add an even more alluring aroma.

Rinse the dried mushrooms, then soak them in the wine for about 1 hour.

Heat 1 tablespoon of the oil in a small roasting tin, add the partridge and brown them all over. Season, then roast in an oven preheated to 230°C/450°F/Gas Mark 8 for 5 minutes. Reduce the oven temperature to 200°C/400°F/Gas Mark 6 and continue cooking for 10–15 minutes, basting once, until done (check as you would for chicken).

Heat the remaining oil in a small saucepan and gently fry the garlic and onion for 5 minutes, until softened. Drain the mushrooms, reserving the liquid. Add the mushrooms to the saucepan and fry for 5 minutes, stirring. Increase the heat, sprinkle in the flour and cook for 1 minute. Stir in the reserved mushroom-soaking liquid and the cream, simmer for 4–5 minutes, then remove from the heat. Season with salt and pepper and add the parsley. Stir in a dash of Madeira or truffle oil, to taste.

Serve the partridge with the mushroom sauce. Broccoli and sauté potatoes or pappardelle pasta make good accompaniments.

## SERVES 2

20g/¾oz dried porcini mushrooms (ceps)

100ml/3½fl oz white wine

2 tablespoons olive oil

2 oven-ready partridge

2 garlic cloves, chopped

¼ onion, finely chopped

1 heaped teaspoon flour

2 tablespoons double cream

1 tablespoon chopped fresh flat-leaf parsley

a dash of Madeira or truffle oil (optional)

salt and freshly ground black pepper

# Leg of lamb with cumin, mint and lemon

This lamb smells and tastes wonderfully fragrant, with its cumin, mint and lemon rub. In winter, serve it with gravy; in summer, simply with the pan juices. Roast fennel (see below) and buttered couscous with some chopped fresh coriander stirred in make good accompaniments.

Pat the meat dry with kitchen paper, then prick it all over with a sharp knife and place in a non-metallic container. Mix together the mint, lemon juice, cumin, olive oil and plenty of black pepper, then rub all over the meat. Place in the refrigerator for at least 6 hours, preferably overnight.

Remove the meat about 30 minutes before cooking and transfer to a large roasting tin. Sprinkle with sea salt and spoon over the marinade. Roast in an oven preheated to 200°C/400°F/Gas Mark 6 for 20 minutes, then reduce the temperature to 180°C/350°F/Gas Mark 4 and cook for a further 20 minutes per 450g/1lb, basting every hour.

When the meat is done to your liking, leave it to rest for 15–20 minutes, then carve and serve with the pan juices.

## SERVES 6–8

| |
|---|
| 1 large leg of lamb, weighing about 3kg/6½lb |
| 15g/½oz fresh mint, finely chopped |
| juice of 2 lemons |
| 1 heaped tablespoon ground cumin |
| 3 tablespoons olive oil |
| sea salt and freshly ground black pepper |

# Roast fennel

Be sure to turn the fennel during cooking or it will brown only on one side.

Trim the top of the fennel and remove any tough outer layers. Cut the fennel into quarters and rinse under cold running water, then pat dry thoroughly. Place in a small roasting dish and pour over the oil. Season with salt and pepper and turn the fennel pieces to coat them well in the oil. Roast in an oven preheated to 230°C/450°F/Gas Mark 8 for about 25 minutes or until tender, basting and turning once. Serve warm, with the pan juices.

## SERVES 6

| |
|---|
| 3–4 large fennel bulbs |
| 5–6 tablespoons olive oil |
| salt and freshly ground black pepper |

| Easter sunday lunch | | Joanna's wine notes |
|---|---|---|
| **Baked truffled eggs** | 67 | Eggs can be tricky with wine but if you happen to be drinking vintage Champagne as your aperitif it will go nicely. The lamb offers an ideal opportunity for a Cabernet Sauvignon-based wine. You could drink a classic Bordeaux but, with the cumin, spice and mint, a fruity New World Cabernet, from Coonawarra (Australia) or Chile, would be better. |
| **Leg of lamb with cumin, mint and lemon** | | |
| **Roast fennel** | | |
| **Chocolate-crusted lemon tart** | 174 | |

Leg of lamb with cumin, mint and lemon,
Roast fennel

# Marinated Brussels sprouts with pecans

## SERVES 6–8

500g/1lb 2oz Brussels sprouts, trimmed

4 tablespoons olive oil

juice of 2 lemons

a good pinch of cayenne pepper

1 garlic clove, crushed

a dash of Angostura bitters

25g/1oz pecan nuts

salt and freshly ground black pepper

**Is there anyone out there who can, hand on heart, actually claim to adore Brussels sprouts? They are, on the whole, something we put up with (wo)manfully each year on 25 December. But if Brussels are treated in a different manner – not boiled to death but served in a tangy marinade – then I am happy to announce that they are more than just good for you.**

If the Brussels sprouts are large, cut them in half. Then steam or boil them until just tender and still vivid green. Refresh briefly under cold running water and pat thoroughly dry.

Whisk together the olive oil, lemon juice, cayenne pepper, garlic and Angostura bitters and season with salt and pepper. Add extra Angostura if you like. Pour this mixture over the still-warm Brussels and toss to coat. Leave to cool and then refrigerate overnight. Bring to room temperature well before serving. Scatter over the nuts.

If you have bought too many Brussels sprouts, use them instead of cabbage to make coleslaw.

# Swedish roast lamb with coffee and cream

## SERVES 6

1 tablespoon olive oil

1 leg of lamb, weighing about 2.5kg/5½lb

1 onion, peeled and cut into quarters

300ml/10fl oz hot, strong black coffee (unsweetened)

25g/1oz butter

25g/1oz plain flour

300ml/10fl oz hot lamb stock

1 heaped tablespoon crème fraîche

1 teaspoon redcurrant jelly

salt and freshly ground black pepper

**I realize this recipe sounds really bizarre but, believe me, it is divine – dark, rich, creamy and delicious. Serve with new potatoes and some green vegetables.**

Heat the oil in a roasting tin on the hob, then add the lamb and onion and brown all over. Transfer to an oven preheated to 220°C/425°F/Gas Mark 7 and roast for 40 minutes. Remove from the oven and pour the hot coffee all over. Reduce the oven temperature to 180°C/350°F/Gas Mark 4 and continue roasting for about an hour or until the meat is done to your liking. Remove the lamb from the roasting tin and keep warm.

Strain off the liquid from the roasting tin and reserve. Place the tin over a direct heat and melt the butter in it, then add the flour. Cook for 1 minute, stirring. Gradually add the strained liquid and the hot stock and cook for 3 minutes, whisking constantly. Stir in the crème fraîche and redcurrant jelly, season to taste and serve with the carved lamb.

# Rumbledethumps with haggis

Although traditionally served only with neeps and tatties (well, all right, also with a ridiculous volume of whisky), haggis is also good with this Lowland Scots dish of potatoes, swede and cabbage. It can be prepared in advance and so lets you get on with your pre-prandial whisky tasting. (Not a good idea, in my opinion, if you want the food to be on the table on time.)

To heat the haggis – which, don't forget, is already cooked – prick it all over, place in an ovenproof dish, cover loosely with foil and place in an oven preheated to 180°C/350°F/Gas Mark 4 for 45–60 minutes.

Cook the potatoes and swede in boiling water until tender, then drain thoroughly. Gently cook the cabbage in 50g/1¾oz of the butter until tender but still vivid green (I melt the butter in a microwave bowl, toss in the cabbage, then cover and microwave for about 3 minutes).

Tip the cabbage and butter into the saucepan of potatoes and swede and mash together with the remaining butter. Season with salt and pepper, then place in an ovenproof dish. Top with the cheese, cover and bake in an oven preheated to 180°C/350°F/Gas Mark 4 for 25 minutes. Remove the lid and cook for a further 15–20 minutes, until piping hot. Serve with the haggis.

## SERVES 4

| |
|---|
| 1 large haggis |
| 600g/1lb 5oz potatoes, peeled and chopped |
| 400g/14oz swede (Scottish turnip), peeled and chopped |
| 250g/9oz cabbage, preferably Savoy, finely sliced |
| 75g/2¾oz butter |
| 25g/1oz Cheddar cheese, grated |
| salt and freshly ground black pepper |

# Haggis-stuffed mushrooms

Serve this for lunch or as a substantial starter. It can even be offered to vegetarians if you use a vegetarian haggis. Unlike the real thing, which is full of bits from inside the sheep, the veggie one is full of nuts, beans and lentils. Take your pick.

Remove the stalks from the mushrooms and chop them finely. Fry with the garlic in a little olive oil until softened.

Cut open the haggis and spoon the contents into a bowl. Combine with the garlic mixture. Pile on to the mushrooms, place in an oiled dish and drizzle with a little olive oil. Bake in an oven preheated to 200°C/400°F/Gas Mark 6 for about 20 minutes or until the mushrooms are soft. Serve at once, with a tiny splash of olive oil over the top.

## SERVES 4

| |
|---|
| 4 large flat-cap mushrooms |
| 3 garlic cloves, chopped |
| olive oil |
| 350g/12oz haggis |

**P**uddings – aah, bliss! Now I am on one of my favourite subjects. I shall lay my cards on the table right now and admit that I have a sweet tooth. I love everything to do with puddings and desserts, whether it is hot or cold, fruity, nutty or chocolatey. I do, therefore, have to fend off an insidious bout of sulks if, after dinner out, all I am offered for dessert is a fruit salad. Much as I adore fresh fruit, it is not quite what I have in mind to assuage that innate craving for a thoroughly sweet finale.

No, I would rather eat something completely excessive and flamboyant than a measly little dish of fruit salad. Where I come from, pudding is taken very seriously; it is not merely an afterthought. Having said that, I do not eat puddings every day and fresh fruit is my family's usual midweek option, as sweet things should be regarded as treats from a dietary and dental point of view. But I must confess that, on a pudding-free night, I have been known to raid the children's special supplies of chocolate when they are in bed, just to satisfy my urge for something sweet. I have even ... no, I feel too ashamed to talk about some other things I have done when I have needed a chocolate fix.

# CHAPTER TEN
# puddings

# Caramelized apples with melted toffee

## SERVES 4

50g/1¾oz unsalted butter

50g/1¾oz soft light brown sugar

4 dessert apples (preferably Cox's or Braeburn), peeled, cored and cut into slices 1cm/½in thick

grated zest of 1 lemon

150ml/5fl oz double cream

200g/7oz luxury toffees

clotted cream, to serve

**Serving this pudding with clotted cream definitely pushes it over the edge of decency, but it is – like most puddings – a treat!**

Melt the butter in a heavy-based saucepan, add the sugar and stir to dissolve. Add the apple slices and stir gently to coat. Cook over a gentle heat until the apples are tender but still quite firm: about 5–8 minutes. Remove from the heat and stir in the lemon zest.

Meanwhile, pour the double cream into a heavy-based saucepan and bring slowly to the boil. Lower the heat to a simmer and add the toffees. Stirring carefully, heat gently until the toffees have completely melted and the mixture has the consistency of a thick sauce.

To serve, place some apple slices and a small spoonful of the lemony juices into each serving bowl. Top with a drizzle of the warm toffee sauce and some clotted cream.

# Chocolate soufflé-cum-mousse

## SERVES 4

150g/5½oz dark chocolate (55–70% cocoa solids)

2 medium free-range egg yolks, plus 4 medium free-range egg whites

50g/1¾oz caster sugar

**Optional garnishes:**

vanilla ice-cream

cloudberry jam or the seeds of 1 passionfruit or ½ pomegranate

**This chocolate pudding is not only delicious it is also extremely versatile. Once made up, the mixture can be baked at once, to serve as a hot soufflé, or wait around for a couple of hours before being baked. It can also be refrigerated overnight, when it miraculously becomes a dense, fudgy chocolate mousse.**

Melt the chocolate in a microwave or in a bowl set over a pan of hot water. Cool slightly, then beat in the egg yolks. In a separate bowl, whisk the egg whites until stiff. Fold in the sugar and continue whisking until glossy and thick. Gently mix 2 spoonfuls of the whites into the chocolate mixture to loosen it and then carefully fold in the rest. Divide between four 7.5cm/3in ramekins. If you are baking the pudding the ramekins should be buttered first. Place them on a baking tray and either bake at once (for the best rise) or keep in the refrigerator for up to 2 hours. Bake in an oven preheated to 220°C/425°F/Gas Mark 7 for 12 minutes (no more), until puffed up. To serve, make a tiny hole in the top of each soufflé and spoon in some ice-cream. Dot with the jam or seeds.

To serve as mousses, chill the unbaked mixture overnight.

# Banana, toffee and pear crumble

**SERVES 6**

500g/1lb 2oz firm pears, peeled, cored and cut into 5–6 slices each

1 tablespoon light muscovado sugar

1 tablespoon lemon juice

4 bananas, thickly sliced

4 heaped tablespoons *dulce de leche*

**For the topping:**

100g/3½oz plain flour

50g/1¾oz butter

50g/1¾oz porridge oats

25g/1oz walnuts, chopped

50g/1¾oz light muscovado sugar

3 tablespoons sunflower oil

**If you cannot find *dulce de leche* (an Argentinian caramel spread, widely available in supermarkets and delicatessens), then boil up an unopened can of condensed milk for 2½–3 hours instead.**

Place the pears in a saucepan with the sugar and lemon juice. Cover and cook gently for 5–10 minutes, until just tender, then remove the lid and continue to cook for 2–3 minutes. Place the bananas in an ovenproof dish. Top with the *dulce de leche*, spreading it all over. Tip over the pears and any juices.

To make the topping, sift the flour into a bowl and rub in the butter, then stir in the oats, nuts and sugar. Add the oil and combine well. Spread this mixture over the pears and press down gently.

Bake in an oven preheated to 200°C/400°F/Gas Mark 6 for about 45 minutes or until golden brown. Leave for at least 10 minutes, then serve warm with oodles of custard.

# Plums in sloe gin

**SERVES 4**

800g/1lb 12oz ripe but firm plums, halved and stoned

100g/3½oz soft light brown sugar

1 teaspoon vanilla extract

200ml/7fl oz sloe gin

thick cream, to serve

**Plums and sloes come from the same botanical family and are perfectly matched in this simple yet delicious dessert.**

Arrange the plums side by side in a large, shallow ovenproof dish which should be just big enough to hold them in a single layer. Sprinkle them with the sugar. Stir the vanilla extract into the gin and pour on to the plums. Cover tightly and bake in an oven preheated to 180°C/350°F/Gas Mark 4 for about 45 minutes, basting carefully once.

Serve the plums barely warm or at room temperature, with their juices and some thick cream.

To make your own sloe gin, prick 450g/1lb sloes and place in a large jar with 110g/4oz sugar and 750ml/1¼ pints gin. Seal and leave somewhere dark for 3 months, shaking occasionally, then strain.

# Chocolate macadamia pavlova

The most popular pudding in Australia, a pavlova is normally topped with whipped cream and fruit. It should have a lovely marshmallow-like centre and be nicely crisp on the outside. My pavlova is shaped into a basket to hold the filling and so is more crispy meringue than soft, squidgy marshmallow ... delicious nonetheless. It is filled with a rich chocolate cream and some toasted macadamia nuts, just to keep true to the Australian theme.

You could accompany it with a little kumquat compote or baked tamarillo, to cut through the richness.

Whisk the egg whites until stiff, then add half the sugar and whisk until stiff and glossy. Add the remaining sugar with the vanilla, vinegar, cornflour and cocoa and whisk until the mixture is thick and shiny.

Line a baking tray with baking parchment. Spread the meringue on to the paper in a circle about 28–30cm/11–12in in diameter, heaping up the sides a little to form a basket. Bake in an oven preheated to 140°C/275°F/Gas Mark 1 for about 1¼ hours, until pale golden. Carefully turn the pavlova upside down on to a wire rack. Wait for about 5 minutes, then gently peel away the paper (do this while still warm or the paper might stick).

For the filling, bring the cream slowly to the boil in a heavy-based saucepan. As soon as bubbles appear on the surface, remove from the heat and add the chocolate. Wait for 5–10 minutes, then stir to melt the chocolate. Once it has completely dissolved into the cream, stir in the mascarpone. Whisk until smooth, then leave to cool (but don't let it get too cold or it will be stiff). Meanwhile, place the nuts on a baking sheet and roast in an oven preheated to 180°C/350°F/Gas Mark 4 for 9–10 minutes, until turning golden brown. Remove and chop coarsely.

Assemble the pavlova no more than 2 hours in advance: spoon the chocolate filling into the middle of the meringue (you might need to microwave the filling briefly to soften it). Scatter the nuts over the surface and serve in wedges, with some pouring cream.

## SERVES 8

4 medium egg whites

225g/8oz caster sugar

1 teaspoon vanilla extract

1 teaspoon white wine vinegar

1 teaspoon cornflour, sifted

1 teaspoon cocoa powder, sifted

### For the filling:

200ml/7fl oz double cream

200g/7oz dark chocolate (55–70% cocoa solids), chopped

2 tablespoons mascarpone cheese

100g/3½oz unsalted macadamia nuts

# Banana and lime ice-cream with chocolate sauce

**This is possibly the easiest ice-cream recipe ever: frozen bananas whizzed in a blender with cream and lime. That's it – no whipping or beating. Magic.**

Place the unpeeled whole bananas in the freezer for at least 6 hours. Remove and leave for about 15 minutes before peeling carefully with a sharp knife (hold the bananas firmly with a cloth). Chop the flesh into small pieces and place in a blender with the fromage frais, lime zest and juice, lemon juice and half the cream. Process until thick and creamy, stopping the motor a couple of times to stir. Serve immediately or place in the freezer for 30–45 minutes to firm up.

For the sauce, melt the chocolate with the remaining cream and the rum. Do this in a pan set over a very gentle heat or in the microwave on Medium. Whisk until smooth and serve at once with the ice-cream.

## SERVES 6

| |
|---|
| 3 large ripe bananas |
| 2 tablespoons thick fromage frais |
| grated zest and juice of 1 lime |
| 1 tablespoon lemon juice |
| 300ml/10fl oz double cream |
| 150g/5½oz dark chocolate (55–70% cocoa solids), chopped |
| 1 tablespoon rum |

# Black-cap pudding

**Black-cap pudding was originally a boiled batter pudding with a cap of buttery dried currants and mixed peel. My version is a light steamed pudding with a sticky summit of blackcurrant jam. Serve with custard.**

Butter a 1 litre/1¾ pint pudding basin and put the jam in the bottom. Cream together the butter and sugar until light and fluffy. Beat in the eggs, one at a time, adding a little of the flour with each egg. Using a metal spoon, fold in the remaining flour, plus the salt, lemon zest and milk. Once thoroughly combined, spoon the mixture carefully on top of the jam and smooth over the top.

To cover, fold a pleat in a double sheet of buttered foil (to allow room for expansion) and tie it securely over the basin with string. (I always make a handle by threading the string twice from one side to the other, so the pudding is easy to lift.) Scrunch up the foil so it does not sit in the water.

Place the basin in a large saucepan over a low heat, then pour boiling water carefully down the side to come about half way up the basin – the water should be simmering gently rather than boiling furiously. Cover the pan with a tight-fitting lid and steam for 1¾–2 hours, topping up the water level if necessary.

Remove the pudding carefully from the pan and wait for about 10 minutes, then take off the foil and run a knife around the edges of the pudding. Place a serving plate on top and carefully invert, so the pudding ends up upright on the plate with the blackcurrant jam glistening seductively on top.

## SERVES 6

| |
|---|
| 2 heaped tablespoons blackcurrant jam |
| 110g/4oz unsalted butter, softened |
| 110g/4oz caster sugar |
| 2 large eggs |
| 175g/6oz self-raising flour, sifted |
| a pinch of salt |
| grated zest of 1 lemon |
| 2 tablespoons milk |

# Warm berry compote with rose petal ice-cream

**SERVES 4**

125g/4½oz raspberries

125g/4½oz blackcurrants or redcurrants

125g/4½oz blueberries

100ml/3½fl oz gin

50g/1¾oz caster sugar

125g/4½oz strawberries

**For the ice-cream:**

2 unsprayed scented roses

425ml/15fl oz double cream

100g/3½oz icing sugar, sifted

2 tablespoons natural yoghurt

2–3 teaspoons rosewater (available from chemists)

**This ice-cream tastes exotic and perfumed yet is seriously easy to make. Choose scented roses (damask or other old-fashioned varieties are best), either red or deep pink for the best visual effect. Remember that most hothouse roses will have been sprayed, so avoid these at all costs. Pick garden roses soon after they have flowered and long before the petals fall off. Although all rose petals are edible, you should be guided by your nose: if the petals have a strong perfume they will add plenty of alluring fragrance to your recipe.**

For the ice-cream, remove the petals from the roses and very gently rinse them if necessary. Trim off the bitter white part at the base. Place the petals in a heavy-based saucepan with the cream and bring slowly to the boil. As soon as bubbles appear on the surface, remove from the heat and pour into a bowl. When cold, place in the refrigerator for at least 2 hours, preferably overnight. Strain the cream, reserving the petals.

Whip the cream with the icing sugar until it forms soft peaks. Stir in the yoghurt, then add rosewater to taste. Gently fold in the petals. Pour into a freezer container and freeze for at least 5 hours or until solid – you don't even have to whisk it. Transfer to the fridge to soften slightly before serving.

For the compote, place all the ingredients except the strawberries in a saucepan. Heat slowly until the sugar dissolves, then increase the heat and bubble for 1 minute. Remove from the heat and stir in the strawberries. Serve with the ice-cream.

# Quince and vanilla compote

**SERVES 4**

3–4 large quince

juice of 1 lemon

150g/5½oz caster sugar

300ml/10fl oz sweet white wine such as Sauternes (or sweet cider)

150ml/5fl oz water

1 vanilla pod, split

**There is something wonderfully evocative about the aroma of a golden-yellow ripe quince. I become almost transfixed as I inhale the alluring, fragrant scent. This simple compote can be made in the autumn when quince are in the shops. Serve with mascarpone cheese flavoured with a little sifted icing sugar and, if possible, a splash of quince eau de vie.**

Peel and core the quince, then cut them into fairly thick slices and lay them in a baking dish. Squeeze over the lemon juice to prevent discoloration. Then sprinkle over the sugar and add the wine, water and vanilla pod. Cover the dish tightly and bake in an oven preheated to 140°C/275°F/Gas Mark 1 for about 2½ hours, until the quince have turned ruby red and the liquid is thick and syrupy. Serve at room temperature.

# Roasted pears with sesame praline ice-cream

## SERVES 4

4 nashi pears

25g/1oz butter, melted

1 tablespoon soft light brown sugar

**For the ice-cream:**

100g/3½oz granulated sugar

100g/3½oz sesame seeds

3 large egg yolks

50g/1¾oz caster sugar

150ml/5fl oz double cream

350ml/12fl oz full-cream milk

**Nashi (Asian) pears are juicy and crisp-crunchy when raw and hold their shape well when cooked, never becoming mushy. If you can't find nashi pears, use underripe ordinary pears.**

To make the praline for the ice-cream, place the granulated sugar in a small, heavy-based saucepan with 2 tablespoons of cold water. Heat very slowly until the sugar dissolves, then increase the heat to medium and cook, without stirring, for 8–10 minutes, until you have a golden caramel. Remove from the heat, stir in the sesame seeds and pour immediately on to a lightly oiled baking tray. Leave until completely cold, then break into chunks and grind in a food processor until roughly chopped (or place in a plastic bag and crush with a rolling pin).

For the ice-cream, whisk the egg yolks and caster sugar together until pale and thick. Bring the cream and milk slowly to the boil and pour about half of this over the egg mixture, whisking all the time. Then return the mixture to the pan, whisk to combine and cook gently, stirring, until just thick enough to coat the back of a spoon. Strain into a bowl, cover tightly with clingfilm and leave to cool.

Stir the praline into the cold custard mixture, then pour into an ice-cream machine and churn (or pour the mixture into a shallow freezer container, cover and freeze, whisking every hour or so).

Quarter the pears, remove the cores and place in an ovenproof dish. Pour over the melted butter and sprinkle over the sugar. Place in an oven preheated to 220°C/425°F/Gas Mark 7 for about 35 minutes or until tender. Serve with the ice-cream.

# Hot chocolate fudge pudding

## SERVES 6-8

200g/7oz self-raising flour

140g/5oz cocoa powder

200g/7oz caster sugar

75g/2¾oz dark chocolate (55–70% cocoa solids), chopped

40g/1½oz butter, melted

1 medium egg

175ml/6fl oz milk

1 teaspoon vanilla extract

150g/5½oz soft dark brown sugar

450ml/16fl oz very hot water

**This is a fabulous pudding of thick fudge sauce nestling under a light chocolate sponge shot through with rivulets of molten chocolate: a chocoholic's dream come true. Serve with thick pouring cream.**

Sift the flour and 25g/1oz of the cocoa into a bowl and stir in the caster sugar. Add the chopped chocolate. Whisk together the melted butter, egg, milk and vanilla and pour into the dry ingredients. Stir thoroughly, then spoon into a buttered 1.5 litre/2½ pint round ovenproof dish (mine is 20cm/8in in diameter). Sift the remaining cocoa powder into a bowl, mix in the brown sugar and sprinkle it over the pudding. Slowly pour the hot water (which should be just off the boil) all over the top of the pudding. Place at once in an oven preheated to 180°C/350°F/Gas Mark 4 and bake for about 50 minutes (without opening the oven door), until the pudding feels fairly firm and springy to the touch. Leave for 5 minutes, then serve.

# Walnut and quince tart with quince cream

This tart is glazed with quince jelly, which is now widely available. The cream is flavoured with more quince jelly and quince eau de vie, and tastes so absolutely divine that I feel sure even the most reserved guest will clamour to scrape the bowl. If you can't find quince eau de vie, just omit it.

For the pastry, sift the flour into a bowl and rub in the butter, then stir in the caster sugar. Mix together the egg and walnut oil and stir this into the mixture to make a dough. Gather into a ball, wrap in clingfilm and chill for 1 hour, then roll out to fit a 20cm/8in buttered tart tin. Prick all over and chill for at least 2 hours, preferably overnight. Line with foil and fill with baking beans, then bake blind at 200°C/400°F/Gas Mark 6 for 15 minutes. Remove the foil and beans and cook for a further 5 minutes. Remove from the oven and leave to cool, then fill with the walnuts.

Melt the butter, then remove from the heat and stir in the brown sugar, eggs, syrup and lemon zest. Pour this mixture over the nuts and bake at 180°C/350°F/Gas Mark 4 for about 30 minutes, until set.

Melt the quince jelly over a low heat with ½ tablespoon of water. Glaze the tart immediately it is out of the oven with some of the melted jelly.

Beat the mascarpone until soft and then add the remaining melted jelly and the eau de vie. Whisk until smooth. Serve the tart warm, with a dollop of the quince cream.

## SERVES 6

| |
| --- |
| 200g/7oz walnuts, chopped |
| 100g/3½oz butter |
| 50g/1¾oz soft light brown sugar |
| 2 medium eggs |
| 2 tablespoons golden syrup |
| grated zest of 1 lemon |
| 4 tablespoons quince jelly |
| 250g/9oz mascarpone cheese |
| 1 tablespoon quince eau de vie |

**For the pastry:**

| |
| --- |
| 175g/6oz plain flour |
| 90g/3¼oz butter, diced |
| 25g/1oz caster sugar |
| 1 medium egg |
| 2 teaspoons walnut oil |

# Bramble clafoutis

**SERVES 4–6**

40g/1½oz plain flour, sifted

40g/1½oz ground almonds

3 large eggs

75g/2¾oz caster sugar

25g/1oz butter, melted

150ml/5fl oz double cream

2 tablespoons milk

1 tablespoon kirsch (or gin)

400g/14oz brambles (blackberries)

**Based on the wonderful French batter pudding, this recipe is made with brambles instead of the more classic cherries. Eat it either warm or at room temperature.**

Whizz all the ingredients except the brambles in a food processor (or whisk thoroughly with a balloon whisk) until smooth. Strain if there are any lumps.

Butter a 22cm/8¾in gratin dish or shallow ovenproof dish. Place the dish in an oven preheated to 200°C/400°F/Gas Mark 6 for a couple of minutes until very hot. Immediately pour in half the batter, then strew the brambles on top. Pour over the remaining batter. Bake at once for about 30 minutes, until puffy and golden brown. Leave for at least 20 minutes before serving.

# Glögi ice-cream

**SERVES 6–8**

1 bottle of red wine

10–12 cardamom pods

1 cinnamon stick

3–4 cloves

1 heaped tablespoon molasses sugar

100g/3½oz raisins

750ml/1¼ pints good-quality vanilla ice-cream

**During my year living in the north of Finland I experienced the famous Finnish _pikkujoulu_ parties in my town of Kemi, a few miles below the Arctic Circle. Meaning 'little Christmas', _pikkujoulu_ are full of fun, games and food – and _glögi_. This innocuous-tasting hot drink is a mixture of red wine, spices and sugar, served in mugs, with a slug of vodka, some raisins and almonds added to each mug just before serving. One night I was invited to three parties and at each one – not to appear impolite – partook of their own special _glögi_. All I can say is that as I staggered out into minus 30°C and thigh-high snow I felt as warm and snug as toast. The next morning was a different story. And even now, some 20 years later, I still have great difficulty drinking any hot wine drink, whether it is mulled red wine or German _glühwein_.**

**However, this delicious ice-cream is an exception. It is simply a reduced _glögi_ mixture stirred into ice-cream to give a delicious, festive dessert. Serve with biscuits or shortbread.**

Put the wine, spices and sugar in a heavy-based saucepan and bring slowly to the boil. Simmer for about 30 minutes or until the wine has thickened slightly and reduced down to about 100ml/3½fl oz. Strain into a bowl, discarding all the spices. Add the raisins to the bowl of wine and leave until completely cold. Meanwhile, allow the ice-cream to soften, then stir in the cold _glögi_ and raisin mixture. Beat well, until thoroughly incorporated. Pour into a 1 litre/1¾ pint pudding basin and cover. Freeze until solid. (It can be frozen for up to 7 days.)

Transfer the bowl to the refrigerator for about 30 minutes to soften up a little, then turn out and decorate with holly if you like. Serve in wedges with biscuits.

# Layered chocolate and cranberry cream

**SERVES 8–10**

250g/9oz dark chocolate (55–70% cocoa solids), grated

250g/9oz fresh wholemeal breadcrumbs

200g/7oz demerara sugar

2 tablespoons cocoa powder, sifted

1 tablespoon coffee granules

600ml/1 pint double cream

300ml/10fl oz single cream

200ml/7fl oz crème fraîche

250g jar of good-quality cranberry sauce

**This stunning-looking creation should be made in a deep glass bowl to show off the creamy layers of brown, white and ruby red. If you don't have a suitable bowl, either beg, borrow or steal one or use a well-scrubbed goldfish bowl or wide-necked flower vase. Prepare everything 48 hours in advance, to allow the sugary chocolate layers to become gooey and sticky and begin to seep into the creamy cranberry layers.**

In a bowl, mix 200g/7oz of the grated chocolate with the breadcrumbs, sugar, cocoa and coffee.

Whisk together the double and single cream until thick but not stiff: this takes longer than usual because of the single cream. Fold in the crème fraîche.

Put one-third of the chocolate breadcrumbs in a large glass bowl and level the top. Top with one-third of the cream, smoothing it over. Carefully dot with half the cranberry sauce, ensuring it is evenly distributed over the cream. Continue to layer: chocolate breadcrumbs, cream, remaining half of the sauce; then chocolate breadcrumbs, then finally cream. Cover with a double layer of foil and refrigerate for 48 hours.

Sprinkle the remaining grated chocolate over the top and serve in small portions – it is extremely rich.

# Cape gooseberries with double chocolate fondue

**SERVES 2**

100g/3½oz cape gooseberries

150ml/5fl oz double cream

65g/2½oz dark chocolate (minimum 55% cocoa solids), chopped

1 teaspoon brandy

65g/2½oz good-quality white chocolate, chopped

1 teaspoon Grand Marnier or Cointreau

**Cape gooseberries (also known as physalis and Chinese lanterns) are wonderful for dipping, with their little stalks to hold and their parchment-thin papery casings peeled back. If you cannot buy cape gooseberries, then dip chunks of banana or fresh pineapple into the fondue instead.**

Put the cape gooseberries in a bowl. Divide the cream between 2 small microwave-proof bowls. Add the dark chocolate and brandy to one bowl, the white chocolate and liqueur to the other. Microwave uncovered (both bowls at once) at Medium-high (not Full) power for 2–3 minutes, until just beginning to melt. Give them a quick stir, then continue to microwave until completely melted and hot.

To serve, place the cape gooseberries and both bowls of chocolate fondue on the table. Take a cape gooseberry, peel back the papery casing and dip the fruit into one or both bowls.

# Brown bread ice-cream with red wine and caramel sauce

**It is essential to caramelize the breadcrumbs with the sugar before mixing them with the ice-cream base, to achieve that characteristic crunch. The sauce might sound rather unusual but in fact the wine lends a deep, spicy edge to an otherwise extremely sweet caramel sauce. Use Argentinian *dulce de leche*, a thick caramel spread that the South Americans lather on their toast, pancakes, ices and cakes.**

For the ice-cream, mix the breadcrumbs and muscovado sugar together and spread over a grill pan. Grill for 10–12 minutes, stirring every minute, until caramelized and dark golden brown. Watch carefully: it can burn quickly. Leave to cool, then break up the crumbs.

Beat the egg yolks with the rum. In a separate bowl, whisk the egg whites until stiff. Fold the yolks gradually into the whites.

Whisk the cream and icing sugar together until floppy, then fold gently into the egg mixture with the yoghurt. Stir in the cooled caramelized crumbs and combine well. Pour into a freezer container and seal. Freeze for 4–5 hours or until solid. (Unlike most ices, it does not require hourly beating.)

For the sauce, place the wine in a heavy-based saucepan and boil rapidly until reduced by about three-quarters. You should have about 4 tablespoons left. Add the *dulce de leche* and cook over a low heat, whisking constantly, until smooth and piping hot.

Put the ice-cream into the refrigerator to soften. Serve with the hot sauce.

## SERVES 4

| |
|---|
| 125g/4½oz fresh brown breadcrumbs |
| 125g/4½oz light muscovado sugar |
| 3 medium free-range eggs, separated |
| 1 tablespoon dark rum |
| 300ml/10fl oz double cream |
| 65g/2½oz icing sugar, sifted |
| 2 tablespoons natural yoghurt |
| 250ml/9fl oz red wine |
| 225g/8oz *dulce de leche* |

# Warm rhubarb compote with white chocolate sorbet

**This is best made in early spring, with tender, pink, delicately flavoured young rhubarb. The thicker stems of main-crop rhubarb are fine but watch out for any tough fibres.**

For the sorbet, melt the chocolate and glucose together (I do this in a microwave on Medium for 5–6 minutes). Pour in the warm water and whisk until smooth. Leave to cool and then pour into a freezer container. Place in the freezer (on fast-freeze if possible) for about 5 hours, removing after 2 hours, then again after 3, and beating vigorously. (Or churn in an ice-cream machine.)

For the compote, place the rhubarb, sugar and grenadine in a saucepan. Bring slowly to the boil and cook, uncovered, for 3–4 minutes or until the rhubarb is just tender. Remove from the heat, cover and cool to lukewarm. Serve the warm compote with a scoop of sorbet on top.

## SERVES 4

| |
|---|
| 700g/1lb 9oz young rhubarb, chopped |
| 50g/1¾oz caster sugar |
| 3 tablespoons grenadine (or water plus 1 teaspoon vanilla extract) |

**For the sorbet:**

| |
|---|
| 250g/9oz good-quality white chocolate, chopped |
| 140g/5oz liquid glucose (available from chemists) |
| 250ml/9fl oz warm water |

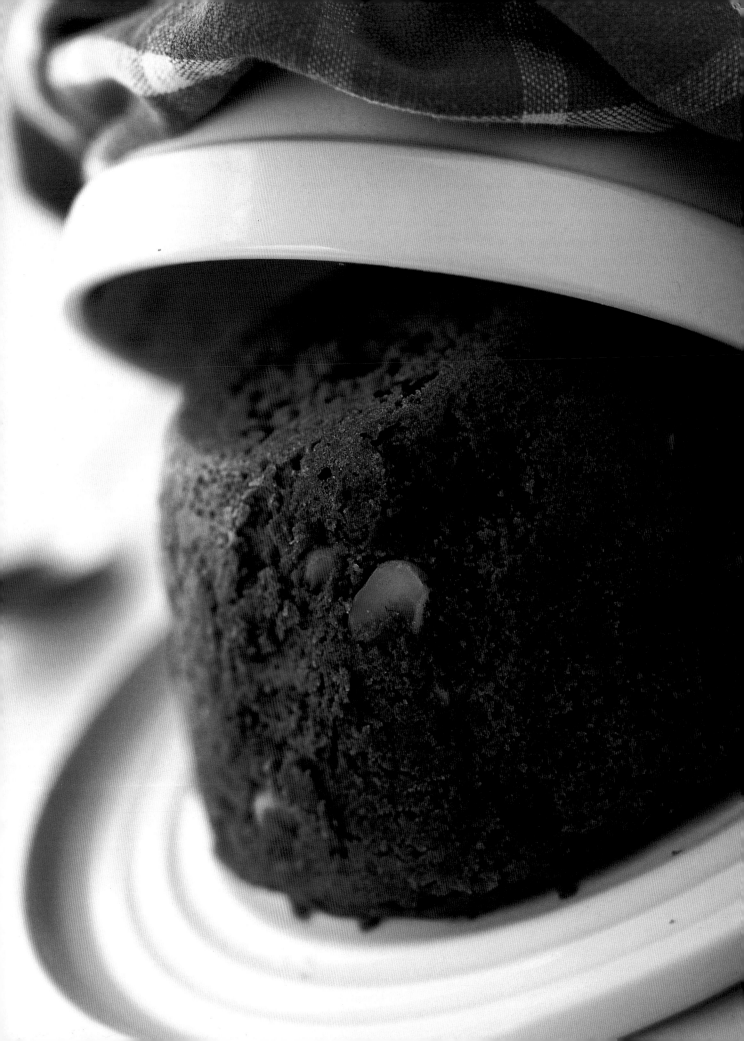

# Chocolate macadamia steamed pudding

This is everything you could wish for in a winter pudding – a couple of hours' eager anticipation as you listen to the rattle of the pudding bowl in the steamer, the glorious puff of steam as it is inverted on to the serving dish, and then the satisfyingly firm yet soft texture of a perfectly cooked steamed sponge pudding. And finally – there is chocolate.

Sift the flour and cocoa together into a bowl. In a separate bowl, cream the butter and sugar together until pale and fluffy, then beat in the eggs, one at a time, adding a little of the flour mixture with the second egg. Fold in the remaining flour mixture and combine gently but thoroughly. Fold in the chocolate and nuts with the milk.

Spoon the mixture into a buttered 1 litre/1¾ pint pudding basin and cover with a double layer of buttered foil, making a pleat in the centre to allow for rising. Tie the foil securely with string, then place in a steamer or in a large saucepan containing enough hot water to come half way up the sides of the basin. Steam for about 1½–2 hours, topping up with hot water if necessary. Remove the foil, loosen the edges of the pudding with a knife and carefully invert on to a serving plate. Serve with pouring cream or Greek yoghurt.

## SERVES 6

| |
|---|
| 175g/6oz self-raising flour |
| 2 heaped tablespoons cocoa powder |
| 125g/4½oz butter, softened |
| 125g/4½oz golden caster sugar |
| 2 large eggs |
| 65g/2½oz dark chocolate (55–70% cocoa solids), chopped |
| 75g/2¾oz unsalted macadamia nuts, toasted and chopped into large chunks |
| 3 tablespoons milk |
| pouring cream or Greek yoghurt |

# Thunder and lightning

This combination of black treacle ice-cream and clotted cream is an extension of the classic Cornish 'thunder and lightning' – black treacle and clotted cream spread on fresh bread or, more commonly, Cornish splits. It is even better served with some thin, lemon-spiked shortbread.

For the ice-cream, put the milk and cream in a saucepan over a low heat. Meanwhile, whisk the egg yolks with the treacle until creamy. Add the salt. Once the milk mixture has nearly reached boiling point, remove from the heat and pour on to the treacle mixture. Whisk well until thoroughly combined, then return to the pan and cook gently, stirring, until it is just thick enough to coat the back of the spoon. Strain into a bowl, cover tightly with clingfilm to prevent a skin forming and leave to cool. Stir in the crème fraîche and whisk well, until blended. Pour into a shallow freezer container and freeze on fast-freeze until it has firmed up – about 4 hours – removing twice and beating vigorously. Alternatively, churn in an ice-cream machine.

Transfer the ice-cream to the refrigerator about 20 minutes before serving. To serve, spoon into bowls and top with a dollop of thick, crusty clotted cream.

## SERVES 4–6

| |
|---|
| 150ml/5fl oz full-cream milk |
| 150ml/5fl oz double cream |
| 4 medium egg yolks |
| 2 tablespoons black treacle |
| a pinch of salt |
| 200ml/7fl oz crème fraîche |
| 225g/8oz clotted cream |

# Chocolate-crusted lemon tart

## SERVES 6

75g/2¾oz dark chocolate (50–60% cocoa solids), grated

3 lemons

4 large eggs, beaten

150g/5½oz golden caster sugar

150ml/5fl oz double cream

icing sugar, to decorate

### For the pastry:

175g/6oz plain flour

25g/1oz cocoa powder

a pinch of salt

25g/1oz icing sugar

125g/4½oz unsalted butter, chilled and diced

1 large egg yolk

2 tablespoons cold water

**Scrub the lemons thoroughly or use unwaxed lemons. Serve the tart at room temperature, with or without cream.**

For the pastry, sift the flour, cocoa powder, salt and icing sugar into a food processor and add the diced butter. Process briefly until blended, then mix together the egg yolk and water and slowly add through the feeder tube. Gather the pastry into a ball, wrap in clingfilm and chill for 1 hour. Then roll out and use to line a 23cm/9in fluted loose-based tart tin. Prick the base with a fork several times and chill for at least 2 hours, preferably overnight. Line with foil and fill with baking beans, then bake blind at 200°C/400°F/ Gas Mark 6 for 15 minutes. Remove the foil and beans and bake for a further 5 minutes, then remove the tart from the oven. Reduce the oven temperature to 170°C/325°F/Gas Mark 3.

While the pastry is still hot, scatter the grated chocolate all over the base. Leave to cool. Grate the lemon zest into a bowl, then squeeze the juice and add to the zest. Add the beaten eggs, sugar and cream and beat until thoroughly combined. Pour this into the pastry case and place it in the oven, taking care that the filling does not spill. Bake for 30–35 minutes, until the filling is just set. Leave to cool completely, then sift over a thin film of icing sugar and cut into slices to serve.

# Mexican bread and butter pudding

## SERVES 4–6

12 slices of baguette, cut 2cm/¾in thick

50g/1¾oz butter, melted

25g/1oz pine nuts, toasted

50g/1¾oz raisins

1 tablespoon black treacle

2 medium eggs

50g/1¾oz dark muscovado sugar

300ml/10fl oz milk

150ml/5fl oz double cream

1 teaspoon ground cinnamon

*Capirotada* is a bread pudding that is often served during the Lenten period in Mexico. Usually made with *bolillos* (little yeast rolls), it is flavoured with almonds or pine nuts, raisins, cinnamon and *piloncillo*, the dark raw sugar of Mexico.

My version of this hearty pudding uses baguette and some black treacle, which gives a similar molasses taste to the Mexican raw sugar. Serve with thick cream.

Arrange half the bread slices in an ovenproof dish and pour over half the melted butter. Sprinkle over half the pine nuts and raisins, then drizzle half the treacle over the top. Make a second layer in the same way.

For the custard, beat together the eggs, sugar, milk, cream and cinnamon, then strain over the bread mixture. Leave to soak for at least 1 hour.

Place in a bain marie (or a roasting pan of hot water) and bake in an oven pre-heated to 170°C/325°F/Gas Mark 3 for 35–40 minutes, until set. Serve warm.

# Strawberry, mint and chocolate brownie trifle

**SERVES 6–8**

500g/1lb 2oz strawberries, hulled

3 tablespoons chopped fresh mint

4 tablespoons freshly squeezed orange juice (or 2 tablespoons orange juice and 2 tablespoons Cointreau)

500g/1lb 2oz mascarpone cheese

100g/3½oz caster sugar

3 large eggs, separated

50g/1¾oz dark chocolate, grated

**For the chocolate brownies:**

150g/5½oz dark chocolate (55–60% cocoa solids)

110g/4oz unsalted butter

4 medium eggs

150g/5½oz caster sugar

110g/4oz plain flour

1 teaspoon baking powder

a pinch of salt

1 teaspoon vanilla extract

**A wicked confection of strawberries, mint, chocolate brownies and mascarpone, this trifle should be made in advance so the layers sink into each other. If you prefer, use good commercial brownies instead of baking your own.**

For the brownies, melt the chocolate and butter together in a microwave or in a pan set over a low heat. Whisk the eggs and sugar together until frothy, then sift in the flour, baking powder and salt. Add the vanilla and stir well. Gently fold in the warm chocolate mixture. Pour into a buttered 23cm/9in square tin and bake in an oven preheated to 180°C/350°F/Gas Mark 4 for 20 minutes. Remove from the oven and cut into 16 squares. Leave in the tin for at least 10 minutes, then transfer to a wire rack to cool.

Set aside a few strawberries for decoration. Roughly chop the rest and mix with the mint and orange juice. Leave to macerate for about 30 minutes.

Beat the mascarpone with the sugar and egg yolks until smooth. Whisk the egg whites until fairly stiff, then stir a little into the mascarpone mixture to lighten it. Gently fold in the rest.

Cut the brownies horizontally in half and place some in a large, deep glass bowl: 4–5 brownies, depending on the size of the base. Top with half the strawberry and mint mixture and juices, which should soak into the brownies. Spread over half of the mascarpone mixture, top with another layer of brownies (you probably will not need them all), then with the remaining strawberries and juices. Finally, spread over the remaining mascarpone. Cover with foil and refrigerate for about 8 hours or overnight. To serve, top with the grated chocolate and the reserved strawberries.

| Be prepared (everything done the night before) | | Joanna's wine notes |
|---|---|---|
| Gazpacho with prawns | 28 | A crisp white Rueda (from Spain) or a Sauvignon Blanc-based wine such as Sancerre would be a good match for the tomato and prawns; but match the creamy lasagne with a rich, buttery Chardonnay or, if you prefer red, a soft Pinot Noir from California or Chile. |
| Chicken and mushroom lasagne | 147 | |
| Strawberry, mint and chocolate brownie trifle | | |

# Nectarine and blueberry slump

**A slump does just that: the light, cobbler-like scones on top slowly slump into the deep puddle of fruit underneath. To make it even more scrumptious, there is a layer of creamy mascarpone between fruit and topping, which melts seductively between the two. Yum.**

Place the blueberries and nectarines in a saucepan with the sugar and orange juice. Heat slowly until the sugar dissolves, then boil for 2 minutes. Remove from the heat. Dissolve the cornflour in 1½ tablespoons of cold water and add this to the fruit. Stirring gently so the berries do not break up, return to the heat and simmer for 3 minutes. Pour into a 20cm/8in round, deep ovenproof dish and leave to cool.

For the topping: shortly before serving, beat the mascarpone until soft and creamy. Using 2 dessertspoons, drop 6 spoonfuls over the fruit, spacing them evenly (take a spoonful of the mixture and scrape it off with the other spoon). Resist the temptation to spread all the blobs together. Sift the flour and baking powder into a bowl and stir in the sugar and orange zest. Make a well in the centre and pour in the juice, then the melted butter. Combine gently but thoroughly. Using the same action as for the mascarpone – with 2 spoons – drop 6 spoonfuls of scone mixture on top of the mascarpone blobs. Do not panic if the scones do not cover it – it is all about to slump anyway.

Bake in an oven preheated to 220°C/425°F/Gas Mark 7 for about 20 minutes, until the fruit is bubbling and the mascarpone oozing out from under the golden-crusted topping. Wait for 5 minutes, then serve.

## SERVES 6

| |
|---|
| 500g/1lb 2oz blueberries |
| 500g/1lb 2oz nectarines, stoned and thinly sliced |
| 75g/2¾oz caster sugar |
| 90ml/3¼fl oz orange juice |
| 20g/¾oz cornflour |

**For the topping:**

| |
|---|
| 250g/9oz mascarpone cheese |
| 175g/6oz self-raising flour |
| 1 teaspoon baking powder |
| 50g/1¾oz caster sugar |
| grated zest and juice of 1 large orange |
| 50g/1¾oz butter, melted and slightly cooled |

# Treacle tart

## SERVES 6

50g/1¾oz fresh white breadcrumbs

grated zest and juice of 1 lemon

6 tablespoons golden syrup

3 tablespoons double cream

**For the pastry:**

125g/4½oz plain flour, sifted

50g/1¾oz ground almonds

25g/1oz golden caster sugar

75g/2¾oz unsalted butter, diced

1 medium egg

**This is not actually treacle tart. It is possibly what you call treacle tart but it is known to many – including myself – as syrup tart. For in Scotland we always distinguish between black treacle and golden syrup. South of the border the difference is often overlooked and so treacle pudding, treacle sponge and treacle tart are in fact made from golden syrup. We make the distinction up North probably because we use black treacle more often than in the South – in gingerbreads, in cloutie dumplings and even spread on bread. At Hallowe'en, we daub it on to scones which are then suspended from a pulley. Children stand underneath and try to bite off as much of the scone as possible. Fortunately there soon follows the other Hallowe'en game of 'dooking for apples', which washes off the fabulously sticky black treacle.**

**Serve this tart (treacle or syrup) warm, with a good slosh of pouring cream.**

For the pastry, place the flour, almonds, sugar and butter in a food processor and process until the mixture resembles breadcrumbs. Add the egg through the feeder tube and process briefly until just combined. Gather together with your hands and wrap in clingfilm. Chill for at least 30 minutes, then roll out to fit a 20cm/8in buttered shallow tart tin (preferably loose-bottomed). Prick all over and chill for at least 3 hours, preferably overnight. Line with foil and baking beans and bake blind in an oven preheated to 200°C/400°F/Gas Mark 6 for 10 minutes, then remove the foil and beans and bake for a further 5 minutes. Remove from the oven and cool briefly.

Mix together the filling ingredients and pour into the pastry case. Bake for 5 minutes, then reduce the oven temperature to 170°C/325°F/Gas Mark 3 and bake for a further 25 minutes or until golden brown and set. Leave to cool for at least 30 minutes and then serve warm with cream.

Once you have rolled out pastry to fit a tart tin it is important to chill it well to prevent shrinkage. Overnight chilling is best – or pop it in the freezer for half an hour.

# Pear and cranberry tarte tatin

**This festive pudding can be made in advance, then simply reheated in a low oven. That means that the potentially hazardous inverting on to the serving dish can be done well before you start on the sherry!**

First make the pastry: place the flour, icing sugar and salt in a food processor. Add the butter and process until the mixture resembles breadcrumbs. Add the egg and just enough cold water to form a stiff dough: begin with 1 tablespoon. Wrap in clingfilm and chill for 1 hour.

For the filling, place a heavy frying pan suitable for both oven and hob (mine is 25cm/10in in diameter and 5cm/2in deep) over a direct heat and melt the butter in it. Add 50g/1¾oz of the sugar and cook, stirring constantly, for about 4–5 minutes or until pale golden brown. Take care the mixture does not burn. Remove from the heat.

Lay the pears on top of the caramelized sugar, arranging them like the spokes of a wheel. Arrange the cranberries in clumps in the middle of the spokes. Sprinkle over the remaining sugar.

Roll out the pastry to a circle about 5cm/2in larger than the pan. Lay this over the pears, carefully tucking the edges between the fruit and the pan. Prick the pastry two or three times with a fork and then bake in an oven preheated to 190°C/375°F/Gas Mark 5 for 40–45 minutes, until golden brown. Remove from the oven and leave to cool for at least 5 minutes, then carefully run a knife around the edges of the pan. Place a large plate on top, hold and invert swiftly. Remove the pan and underneath you should have a perfectly turned-out tarte Tatin. If not, just patch it up. Serve warm, with crème fraîche.

## SERVES 4

50g/1¾oz unsalted butter

75g/2¾oz caster sugar

700g/1lb 9oz pears, peeled, cored and thickly sliced

100g/3½oz cranberries

**For the pastry:**

225g/8oz plain flour, sifted

25g/1oz icing sugar, sifted

a pinch of salt

140g/5oz chilled unsalted butter, diced

1 medium egg

1–2 tablespoons cold water

I was brought up to the homely smells of baking. It was part of growing up. My mother would always have home-baked scones, buns or cakes ready for us returning from school, or for unexpected visitors dropping in. I hardly knew what a shop-bought bun tasted like, while chocolate biscuits were practically unheard of. But I certainly don't think I was deprived, although my own children, who also return from school to tins of home-baked goodies, would simply die for a KitKat.

Although the health lobby would have us believe that cakes, buns, scones and pastries are bad for us, I would suggest that processed (commercial) ones may well be, when pumped full of preservatives and other additives, but that home baking is not necessarily unhealthy, especially when organic ingredients and unrefined sugar are used. And yes, cakes contain fat and sugar, which are not good for us in excess, but at least you – the baker – are the arbiter of how much goes in and whether the ingredients are top-quality.

Turn on your oven right now and start slavering at the thought of those sweet, fragrant aromas emanating from the kitchen and the sight of some light, golden-crusted scones cooling on the rack. All you need to do is a spot of weighing, mixing and cutting out. A little patience as you let them cool also helps.

# CHAPTER ELEVEN

# cakes and bakes

# Crunchy caramel cake

**SERVES 8**

175g/6oz unsalted butter, softened

175g/6oz caster sugar

3 medium eggs

175g/6oz self-raising flour

2 large Crunchie bars

**For the caramel icing and decoration:**

50g/1¾oz unsalted butter

50g/1¾oz light brown sugar

2 tablespoons double cream

150g/5½oz icing sugar, sifted

1 teaspoon vanilla extract

½ Crunchie bar

**This is a light, buttery cake dotted with pieces of Crunchie bar, the chocolate-covered honeycomb bar sold as Violet Crumbles in Australia. It is topped with a thick caramel icing and decorated with more broken Crunchie.**

**Another family favourite is Crunchie pudding, made by whizzing up 2–3 Crunchies in a food processor with the pulse button, then gently folding them into 300ml/10fl oz whipped cream. Spoon into a bowl and leave overnight. The next day you will have a lovely, fudgy, creamy dessert. The taste is not immediately recognizable and it will keep guests guessing for some time.**

Beat together the butter and caster sugar until pale and fluffy: either do this vigorously with a wooden spoon or use an electric beater. Add the eggs one by one, gradually beating them in. If they look as if they might curdle, add a small spoonful of the flour. Once the eggs are fully incorporated, sift in the flour and gently fold it in with a metal spoon. Whizz the Crunchies in a food processor until roughly chopped (or bash them in a plastic bag), then gently fold them into the mixture. Spoon into a buttered, base-lined 23cm/9in round cake tin. Bake in an oven preheated to 180°C/350°F/Gas Mark 4 for 25–30 minutes or until a skewer inserted in the centre of the cake comes out clean. Invert on to a wire rack to cool.

For the icing, melt the butter and brown sugar very slowly in a saucepan, then add the cream. Bring to the boil and, stirring constantly, boil for about 3 minutes. Remove from the heat and beat in the sifted icing sugar and the vanilla. Beat vigorously with a wooden spoon or an electric beater until smooth and spreadable. Spread over the cooled cake. Crush the ½ Crunchie bar and sprinkle it over the top.

# Apple-dapple cake

**My friend Hils, who gave me this recipe, adds a cup of pecans for extra crunch. Serve as a pudding, with plenty of whipped cream or thick yoghurt, or eat it cold, with a cup of tea.**

Whisk together the eggs, oil, caster sugar and water until well combined, then sift in the flour, salt, bicarbonate of soda and cinnamon and stir well. Stir in the vanilla extract and apples. Pour the mixture into a buttered, deep 24cm/9½in loose-bottomed round cake tin and bake in an oven preheated to 180°C/350°F/Gas Mark 4 for 60–70 minutes: test by inserting a skewer into the middle – it should come out clean when the cake is done. Cover loosely with foil towards the end, if necessary, to prevent overbrowning.

Meanwhile, put the muscovado sugar, milk and butter in a saucepan and bring slowly to the boil. Boil for 3–4 minutes until thickened, stirring often. Leave to cool for at least 5 minutes.

Once the cake is cooked, remove from the oven. Slowly pour over the sauce, then return to the oven for 2 minutes. Transfer to a wire rack and run a knife around the edges. Allow to cool in the tin.

## SERVES 8

| |
|---|
| 3 medium eggs |
| 200ml/7fl oz sunflower oil |
| 300g/10½oz golden caster sugar |
| 4 tablespoons cold water |
| 375g/13oz plain flour |
| ½ teaspoon salt |
| 1 teaspoon bicarbonate of soda |
| 1 teaspoon ground cinnamon |
| 2 teaspoons vanilla extract |
| 2 large Bramley apples, peeled, cored and chopped |
| 100g/3½oz light muscovado sugar |
| 3 tablespoons milk |
| 100g/3½oz butter |

# Raspberry crumble cake

**This can be served warm as a pudding with some thick yoghurt or cream, cold with a cup of tea, or as part of a picnic. Substitute blackcurrants for the raspberries if you prefer, but increase the sugar in the crumble by 25g/1oz.**

For the base, place the flour, sugar and butter in a food processor and process briefly until the mixture resembles breadcrumbs. Mix the eggs and lemon juice and slowly add through the feeder tube. Stop the machine and gather the dough together with your hands. Press it over the base of a buttered swiss roll tin (23 x 33cm/9 x 13in) and level the surface.

To make the topping, sift the flour and cinnamon into a bowl and stir in the sugar, then rub in the butter until the mixture is crumbly. Gently toss the raspberries with the semolina, taking care not to break up the fruit. Spoon them over the base, leaving a narrow margin around the edges. Top with the crumble mixture and very gently press it down to cover the raspberries.

Bake in an oven preheated to 200°C/400°F/Gas Mark 6 for about 45 minutes or until the base is cooked and the crumble golden brown. Leave to cool for about 30 minutes, then cut into squares and remove from the tin.

## SERVES 8

| |
|---|
| 150g/5½oz plain flour |
| 2 teaspoons ground cinnamon |
| 100g/3½oz caster sugar |
| 125g/4½oz butter, diced |
| 500g/1lb 2oz raspberries |
| 1 heaped tablespoon semolina |

**For the base:**

| |
|---|
| 350g/12oz plain flour, sifted |
| 2 tablespoons caster sugar |
| 200g/7oz butter, diced |
| 2 medium eggs |
| ½ tablespoon lemon juice |

# White pepper scones with strawberries and clotted cream

**MAKES 8**

225g/8oz self-raising flour

1 level teaspoon baking powder

¼–½ teaspoon ground white pepper

2 teaspoons caster sugar

50g/1¾oz butter, diced

150ml/5fl oz milk

clotted cream and sliced strawberries, to serve

**Since strawberries are often sprinkled with a little white pepper to enhance their sweetness (just like the Italians do in Modena with balsamic vinegar), there seems no reason why you should not flavour the scones for a strawberry cream tea with a little pepper. Glaze the scones with egg yolk for an extra shiny crust.**

Sift the flour and baking powder into a bowl, then add the pepper: ¼ teaspoon if you feel nervous, a scant ½ teaspoon if you want more of a kick. Stir in the caster sugar, then rub in the butter until the mixture resembles breadcrumbs. Add the milk and quickly mix together to form a fairly soft dough. Do not overwork. Bring the dough together with your hands and place on a lightly floured board. Do not knead but gently press the dough out into a circle about 2cm/¾in high. Using a 5cm/2in cutter, cut out into scones, pressing together the trimmings to make 8 scones all together. Place on a lightly buttered baking tray. Bake in an oven preheated to 220°C/425°F/Gas Mark 7 for 12–14 minutes, until well risen. Transfer to a wire rack to cool.

To serve, split the scones and spread the lower halves thickly with clotted cream. Top with as many strawberries as possible then serve, either open or covered with the top half.

> When you are making scones, think happy thoughts; when you are making bread, think of your worst enemy.

# Choc-chip toffee rock cakes

**MAKES 12**

350g/12oz plain flour

1 level tablespoon baking powder

a pinch of salt

100g/3½oz caster sugar

50g/1¾oz dark chocolate chips

100g/3½oz milk chocolate caramel, chopped

200ml/7fl oz plain yoghurt

2 medium eggs, beaten

**These large rock buns are surprisingly light in texture as they are made with yoghurt and eggs, and no fat at all. So you needn't feel guilty about all the chocolate and toffee bits in them! Cadbury's caramel bars are ideal (you'll need two) or any chocolate-covered caramel.**

Sift the flour, baking powder and salt into a bowl. Stir in the sugar, then the chocolate chips and caramel pieces.

Beat together the yoghurt and eggs. Make a well in the centre of the flour mixture and pour this in. Using a wooden spoon, combine gently but thoroughly to a soft dough. Do not overwork. Spoon 12 large blobs on to a buttered baking tray and bake in an oven preheated to 190°C/375°F/Gas Mark 5 for about 20 minutes, until tinged with golden brown. Leave to cool on a wire rack for at least 10 minutes, then devour while warm and gooey.

# Caramel toffee flapjack

**Dulce de leche** is an Argentinian caramel spread now available in good delicatessens and supermarkets. If you cannot find it, however, boil a couple of unopened cans of condensed milk for 2½–3 hours, then open once cold.

First melt together the butter, syrup and sugar – do this either in a microwave or in a saucepan over a low heat. Remove from the heat and stir in the oats, flour and salt until well combined. Pour the mixture into a buttered swiss roll tin (23 x 33cm/9 x 13in) and bake in an oven preheated to 180°C/350°F/Gas Mark 4 for 20–25 minutes, until golden brown. Do not allow it to become too dark at the edges.

Meanwhile, warm the *dulce de leche* up a little (it will spread over the base more easily once warm). I simply place the unlidded jar in a microwave on Medium for a couple of minutes. Alternatively spoon it into a saucepan and heat gently. Immediately the base is out of the oven, pour the caramel on top and spread it gently all over. Leave to cool.

Once cool, melt the chocolate in a microwave or in a basin set over a pan of hot water. Pour it over the caramel, again gently spreading it out to cover completely. Leave until cold before cutting into squares.

**MAKES 24**

| |
|---|
| 200g/7oz unsalted butter |
| 4 level tablespoons golden syrup |
| 50g/1¾oz demerara sugar |
| 300g/10½oz porridge oats |
| 100g/3½oz self-raising wholemeal flour |
| a pinch of salt |
| 450g jar of *dulce de leche* |
| 200g/7oz dark chocolate (55–60% cocoa solids) |

# Sticky pecan brownies

**You can substitute walnuts or macadamias for the pecans if you like. And you can top the brownies with a rich chocolate frosting to make them even richer. But I like them as they are, served barely warm, with a blob of ice-cream.**

Gently melt the chocolate and butter together, then leave to cool for about 5 minutes. Meanwhile, beat the eggs and sugar together with a whisk until creamy. Fold in the flour, baking powder, salt and vanilla, then gently fold in the chocolate mixture and pecans. Stir well, but not too vigorously, to mix everything. Pour into a buttered 23cm/9in square tin and bake in an oven preheated to 180°C/350°F/Gas Mark 4 for 20 minutes: test by inserting a skewer in the middle; it should come out with a little mixture adhering to it. Cut into squares at once, then leave to cool for at least 15 minutes before decanting. Using a spatula, carefully transfer the squares to a wire rack and cool for a further 15 minutes or so.

**MAKES 16**

| |
|---|
| 150g/5oz dark chocolate (minimum 50% cocoa solids) |
| 125g/4½oz unsalted butter |
| 3 large eggs, beaten |
| 175g/6oz light soft brown sugar |
| 125g/4½oz plain flour, sifted |
| 1 teaspoon baking powder |
| a pinch of salt |
| 1 teaspoon vanilla extract |
| 50g/1¾oz pecan nuts, roughly chopped |

**Caramel toffee flapjack,
Mincemeat polenta crumble bars (page 188),
Sticky pecan brownies**

# Warm date cake with coconut fudge topping

**SERVES 6**

175g/6oz dates, stoned and chopped

250ml/9fl oz warm water

1 teaspoon bicarbonate of soda

65g/2½oz butter, melted

1 medium egg, beaten

1 teaspoon vanilla extract

175g/6oz caster sugar

175g/6oz plain flour, sifted

1 teaspoon baking powder

**For the topping:**

150g/5½oz dark muscovado sugar

65g/2½oz butter

150g/5½oz desiccated coconut

3 tablespoons milk

**This scrumptious cake is easy as it is made in just one saucepan. The batter is mixed in the pan, then poured into a cake tin to bake. Meanwhile, the ingredients for the coconut fudge topping are heated in the same – unwashed – pan and spooned over the cake 10 minutes before the end of cooking. The result is a sticky, nutty topping on a light, date-studded cake (and minimal washing up).**

Put the dates, water and bicarbonate of soda in a heavy saucepan. Heat slowly until the dates are soft – about 5–10 minutes. Remove from the heat and add the melted butter, egg, vanilla extract, sugar, flour and baking powder. Stir well, then pour the mixture into a buttered deep 18cm/7in loose-bottomed round cake tin. Bake in an oven preheated to 180°C/350°F/Gas Mark 4 for 20 minutes.

Meanwhile, put all the topping ingredients into the same (unwashed) saucepan. Heat gently until the sugar has dissolved and the butter melted. Then increase the heat to medium and cook, stirring, for about 2–3 minutes.

After the cake has baked for 20 minutes, remove it from the oven and carefully spoon the topping mixture over it, spreading it out gently. Return to the oven and cook for a further 10–12 minutes, until the topping is golden brown. Leave to cool for 20–30 minutes, then carefully turn out on to a serving plate. Serve warm with thick cream.

# Mincemeat polenta crumble bars

**MAKES 20–24**

200g/7oz plain flour

50g/1¾oz icing sugar

75g/2¾oz polenta

200g/7oz butter, diced

300g/10½oz mincemeat

**Cut into dainty squares, these make an interesting alternative to mince pies around Christmas. Throughout the rest of the year I cut them into larger bars and use them for picnics, lunch-boxes and tea-time. Be sure to use the best mincemeat you can find – home-made if possible.**

Sift the flour and icing sugar into a bowl, then stir in the polenta. Rub in the butter until the mixture resembles breadcrumbs. Add enough cold water to bind it together in a fairly loose dough – 3–4 tablespoons. Press about two-thirds of this mixture into a buttered 23cm/9in square baking tin. Spread over the mincemeat, leaving a margin all around. Dip your fingers in flour, then crumble over the remaining mixture, pressing it down gently.

Bake in an oven preheated to 190°C/375°F/Gas Mark 5 for 30 minutes, until golden brown. Remove from the oven and cut into 20–24 pieces. Leave to cool in the tin.

# Chocolate cake with fig and chocolate cream

**This is a polenta chocolate cake topped with a fig- and Marsala-flavoured chocolate ganache. It is rich, creamy and worryingly moreish. Refrigerate any leftovers for the next day.**

Cream the sugar and butter together until light and fluffy. Melt the chocolate in a microwave or in a basin set over a pan of hot water. Beat the egg yolks into the butter mixture, then stir in the chocolate. Fold in the polenta, flour and cocoa. In a separate bowl, whisk the egg whites until stiff and then fold them gradually into the cake mixture. Pour into a buttered 24cm/9½in loose-bottomed round cake tin and bake in an oven preheated to 180°C/350°F/ Gas Mark 4 for about 30 minutes, until just firm to the touch. Transfer to a wire rack, remove the side of the tin and leave to cool.

For the fig cream, soak the figs in the Marsala for about 30 minutes. Place the cream in a saucepan and bring slowly to the boil. As soon as bubbles appear on the surface, remove from the heat and add the chocolate. Stir until the chocolate has completely melted, then stir in the mascarpone. Whisk until smooth, then add the figs and all their liquor and combine everything well.

Once the cake is cool, remove from the base and place on a plate. Top with the fig cream.

## SERVES 8

150g/5½oz golden caster sugar

150g/5½oz unsalted butter

100g/3½oz dark chocolate (55–70% cocoa solids)

3 large eggs, separated

50g/1¾oz fine polenta

50g/1¾oz self-raising flour, sifted

25g/1oz cocoa powder, sifted

### For the fig and chocolate cream:

150g/5½oz dried figs, stems removed, roughly chopped

2 tablespoons Marsala

200ml/7fl oz double cream

200g/7oz dark chocolate (55–70% cocoa solids)

2 heaped tablespoons mascarpone cheese

## Afternoon tea

**Smoked salmon and cucumber sandwich loaf**   100

**White pepper scones with strawberries and clotted cream**   184

**Treacle tart**   178

**Chocolate cake with fig and chocolate cream**

## Joanna's wine notes
You could drink Champagne with the smoked salmon, Sauternes with the scones and tawny port with the chocolate cake, but wouldn't a cup of Darjeeling be nice?

# index

aïoli, Roasted garlic 143
Algerian guinea fowl with avocado relish 109
Anchovy & spinach tart 68, *69*
apples
    Apple-dapple cake 183
    Caramelized, with melted toffee 158
    Hot pork & apple loaf *78, 79*
    Roast pork with cinnamon apples 144, *145*
artichokes
    Artichoke, rocket & Parmesan salad 40
    Tuna, artichoke & mushroom cobbler 92
Asparagus with herb mayo, toasted
    hazelnuts & Parmesan 23
Asparagus with soft-boiled eggs 77
aubergines
    Aubergine & feta cheese rolls 16
    Aubergine & feta sandwich 74, *75*
    Aubergine & mozzarella stack with
        salsa verde 132
    Chicken, aubergine & aïoli sandwich 93
    Grilled, with sweet chilli paste 20
    Roasted ratatouille vinaigrette *18, 19*
    Turkish aubergine dip with garlic & dill 19
avocados
    Algerian guinea fowl with avocado relish 109
    Bacon, avocado & papaya salad 50, *51*
    Chilled avocado soup with chilli jam 30
    Prawn, avocado & cheese quesadillas 79
    Warm smoked salmon, Brie & avocado
        croissants 55

Bacon, avocado & papaya salad 50, *51*
Bagels with lox & cream cheese 54
Baked tomato eggs 76
Baked truffled eggs 67
Banana & lime ice-cream with chocolate
    sauce *162, 163*
Banana pancakes with maple syrup 62
Banana, toffee & pear crumble 160
Barbecued mushrooms with anchovy
    mayonnaise 101
Barbecued mussels in foil *110*, 111
Barley risotto 84
beans *see* black beans; butter beans
beef
    Meatloaf with roasted hazelnut
        & tomato sauce 118
    Shepherd's pie with parsnip topping 125
    *see also* steak
Beetroot & ginger chutney 105
Beetroot & red wine risotto 90, *91*
black beans
    Beef with black bean sauce & noodles 88
    Black bean & red pepper salad 44
Black-cap pudding 163
Black olive salsa *86*, 87
black pudding, Pork casserole with
    black pudding crust 121
blackcurrants
    Roast grouse with blackcurrants 140
    Warm berry compote with rose petal
        ice-cream 164, *165*
blueberries
    Nectarine & blueberry slump 177
    Panettone French toast with
        orange-fried blueberries 57
    Warm berry compote with rose petal
        ice-cream 164, *165*
Bramble clafoutis 168, *169*
bread
    Bush bread with beer 108
    Oregano cornbread 72
    Potato & herb 72
    Walnut, with goat's cheese 71
bread & butter pudding, Mexican 174
Brown bread ice-cream with red wine
    & caramel sauce 171

brownies
    Sticky pecan *186*, 187
    Strawberry, mint & chocolate brownie trifle 176
bruschetta, Tomato & Marmite 68
Brussels sprouts, Marinated, with pecans 154
Bush bread with beer 108
Butter bean & parsley salad 44

cabbage
    Cabbage soup with a cheese & mustard
        crust 37
    Rumbledethumps with haggis 155
    Salmon fillets with stir-fried cabbage
        & roasted garlic aïoli 143
Caesar salad 47
cakes
    Apple-dapple 183
    Caramel toffee flapjack *186*, 187
    Choc-chip toffee rock 184
    Chocolate, with fig & chocolate cream 189
    Crunchy caramel 182
    Mincemeat polenta crumble bars *186*, 188
    Raspberry crumble 183
    Warm date, with coconut fudge topping 188
    White pepper scones with strawberries
        & clotted cream 184, *185*
Calzone with Taleggio, garlic & spinach 76
Cape gooseberries with double  chocolate fondue
    170
Caramel toffee flapjack *186*, 187
Caramelized apples with melted toffee 158
Cauliflower cheese soup 26
ceviche
    Pacific 22
    Scallop 12
Chargrilled chicken & tapenade on sourdough 100
cheese
    Aubergine & feta cheese rolls 16
    Aubergine & feta sandwich 74, *75*
    Aubergine & mozzarella stack with
        salsa verde 132
    Bagels with lox & cream cheese 54
    Cabbage soup with a cheese &
        mustard crust 37
    Calzone with Taleggio, garlic & spinach 76
    Cauliflower cheese soup 26
    Cheese-stuffed rice balls *137*, 138
    Chicken breasts with spinach, tomato &
        mozzarella 84
    Chicory & Gruyère tart 132
    Feta, mangetout & olive crumble 97
    Fresh tomato & feta penne 115
    Goat's cheese, thyme & black olive gratin 22
    Hot pork & apple loaf *78*, 79
    Lamb & tomato crêpe stack 126, *127*
    Leeks with mustard & cheese 80
    Mushroom pizza *96*, 97
    Parmesan snaps 138
    Prawn, avocado & cheese quesadillas 79
    Saffron & manchego tartlets 136, *137*
    Spinach & goat's cheese soufflé 13
    Spinach empanadas 104
    Steak & chips with Roquefort butter 89
    Stilton & pear salad 20, *21*
    Stuffed spicy sea bass 105
    Walnut bread with goat's cheese 71
    Warm smoked salmon, Brie &
        avocado croissants 55
chicken
    Chargrilled chicken & tapenade
        on sourdough 100
    Chicken & mushroom lasagne 147
    Chicken, aubergine & aïoli sandwich 93
    Chicken breasts with spinach, tomato &
        mozzarella 84
    Chicken with a coriander & walnut
        crust & fried capers 90

    Chicken with pesto & tomato & basil sauce
        119
    Chicken with preserved lemons &
        black olives *130*, 131
    Herb & mustard roast 133
    Spicy chicken kebabs 108
    Sweet potato mash with yassa chicken 114
    Tom yam soup 31
Chicken livers with toasted brioche & gherkins 74
Chicory & Gruyère tart 132
Chilled avocado soup with chilli jam 30
Chilli 20,30
chilli, Venison 116, *117*
Chinese noodle salad with mango, crab & ginger
    *148, 149*
chocolate
    Banana & lime ice-cream with
        chocolate sauce *162, 163*
    Cape gooseberries with double
        chocolate fondue 170
    Caramel toffee flapjack *186*, 187
    Choc-chip toffee rock cakes 184
    Chocolate cake with fig & chocolate cream 189
    Chocolate-crusted lemon tart 174, *175*
    Chocolate macadamia pavlova 161
    Chocolate macadamia steamed
        pudding *172, 173*
    Chocolate soufflé-cum-mousse 158, *159*
    Hot chocolate fudge pudding 166
    Layered chocolate & cranberry cream 170
    Sticky pecan brownies *186*, 187
    Strawberry, mint & chocolate brownie trifle 176
    Warm rhubarb compote with white
        chocolate sorbet 171
chowder, Clam, in a sourdough breadbowl *32*, 33
chutney, Beetroot & ginger 105
clafoutis
    Bramble 168, *169*
    Tomato & pesto 94
Clam chowder in a sourdough breadbowl *32*, 33
cobbler, Tuna, artichoke & mushroom 92
coconut
    Grenadian spinach & coconut soup 34
    Prawns with coconut 66
    Roast cod with a coconut & lime sauce &
        mango salsa 146
    Warm date cake with coconut
        fudge topping 188
cod
    Cod with black olive salsa *86*, 87
    Roast, with a coconut & lime sauce
        & mango salsa 146
compotes
    Quince & vanilla 164
    Warm berry, with rose petal ice-cream
        164, *165*
    Warm rhubarb, with white chocolate
        sorbet 171
Corned beef hash 56, 57
cornmeal
    Mealie meal muffins 61
    Oregano cornbread 72
    *see also* polenta
Courgette & mint tortilla 101
Courgettes with garlic & cream 77
couscous, Mint couscous tabbouleh 49
crab
    Chinese noodle salad with mango, crab &
        ginger *148, 149*
    Crab & dill pasta 89
cranberries
    Cranberry cinnamon muffins *60*, 61
    Layered chocolate & cranberry cream 170
    Pear & cranberry tarte tatin 179
Creamed mushroom soup with soy 27
crêpes
    Lamb & tomato crêpe stack 126, *127*

Mussel & saffron 124
croissants, Warm smoked salmon, Brie &
    avocado 55
crumbles
    Banana, toffee & pear 160
    Feta, mangetout & olive 97
    Raspberry crumble cake 183
Crunchie pudding 182
Crunchy caramel cake 182
curd, Lemon 63

dates, Warm date cake with coconut
    fudge topping 188
dip, Turkish aubergine, with garlic & dill 19
Duck & orange salad 46, 47
Duck with orange-roasted radicchio 140
dulce de leche
    Banana, toffee & pear crumble 160
    Brown bread ice-cream with red wine &
        caramel sauce 171
    Caramel toffee flapjack 186, 187

eggs
    Asparagus with soft-boiled eggs 77
    Baked tomato eggs 76
    Baked truffled eggs 67
    Poached eggs on pesto toast 70, 71
    Scrambled eggs with Parma ham 54
    see also dishes made with eggs
        e.g. omelettes, soufflés
empanadas, Spinach 104

fennel, Roast 152, 153
Feta, mangetout & olive crumble 97
figs
    Chocolate cake with fig & chocolate cream 189
    Rabbit with green olives, figs & polenta 128
fish & seafood
    Fish in Asian broth 28
    Fishcakes with salmon roe & soured cream 129
    Luxury fish pie with prawns 122, 123
    Pacific ceviche 22
    Thai fish balls with dipping sauce 73
    Thai seafood salad 48
    see also by name e.g. prawns, salmon
flapjack, Caramel toffee 186, 187
fondue, Cape gooseberries with double
    chocolate fondue 170
French toast, Panettone, with orange-fried
    blueberries 57
Fresh tomato & feta penne 115

Gazpacho with prawns 28, 29
Glögi ice-cream 168
Goat's cheese, thyme & black olive gratin 22
Granary picnic loaf with salami &
    grilled peppers 102, 103
Granola 58
gratins
    Goat's cheese, thyme & black olive 22
    Herring 116
    Juniper 141
Grenadian spinach & coconut soup 34
Grilled aubergines with sweet chilli paste 20
grouse, Roast, with blackcurrants 140
guacamole, Oysters with guacamole 17
guinea fowl, Algerian, with avocado relish 109

haggis
    Haggis-stuffed mushrooms 155
    Rumbledethumps with haggis 155
Ham & spinach omelette 55
hash, Corned beef 56, 57
Hawker's spicy noodles 94, 95
hazelnuts
    Asparagus with herb mayo, toasted
        hazelnuts & Parmesan 23
    Meatloaf with roasted hazelnut &
        tomato sauce 118
    Pancetta & fig salad with hazelnut dressing 41
Herb & mustard roast chicken 133
Herring gratin 116
Hot chocolate fudge pudding 166
hot dogs, Tortilla 104
Hot pork & apple loaf 78, 79

ices & ice-creams 162, 163-4, 165, 166, 168,
    171, 173

jam
    Chilli 30
    Raspberry, with Drambuie 63
Juniper gratin 141

kebabs, Spicy chicken 108

lamb
    Lamb & quince tagine 115
    Lamb & tomato crêpe stack 126, 127
    Leg of, with cumin, mint & lemon 152, 153
    Slow-braised lamb shanks 120, 121
    Swedish roast, with coffee & cream 154
Layered chocolate & cranberry cream 170
Leeks with mustard & cheese 80
Leg of lamb with cumin, mint & lemon 152, 153
lemon
    Chicken with preserved lemons &
        black olives 130, 131
    Chocolate-crusted lemon tart 174, 175
    Leg of lamb with cumin, mint & lemon 152, 153
    Lemon curd 63
    Mushroom, lemon & noodle soup 34, 35
    Pasta with lemon & cream 14
    Stuffed squid with lemon oil 133
Lemongrass mayonnaise 16
Lentil & ginger soup 30
Luxury fish pie with prawns 122, 123

macadamia nuts
    Chocolate macadamia pavlova 161
    Chocolate macadamia steamed
        pudding 172, 173
mangetout, Feta, mangetout & olive crumble 97
mango
    Chinese noodle salad with mango,
        crab & ginger 148, 149
    Mango salsa 146
    Pheasant breasts with mango sauce 139
    Roast cod with a coconut & lime sauce &
        mango salsa 146
Marinated Brussels sprouts with pecans 154
Marinated tuna with roasted tomato relish 106,
    107
mayonnaise 16, 23, 101, 143
Mealie meal muffins 61
Meatloaf with roasted hazelnut & tomato sauce
    118
melon, Smoked venison with melon 14, 15
menus
    Afternoon tea 189
    Autumn dinner 36
    Barbecue party 106
    Be prepared 176
    Boxing Day buffet 149
    Cocktail party 136
    Easter Sunday lunch 153
    Family picnic 102
    Family Sunday lunch 144
    Festive brunch party 54
    Quick weekend supper 14
    Salad days 45
    Spring lunch 143
    Storecupboard supper 85
    Summer supper 49
    Tropical lunch 66
    Valentine's dinner 33
    Winter supper 224
Mexican bread & butter pudding 174
Mincemeat polenta crumble bars 186, 188
Mint couscous tabbouleh 49
monkfish, Roast, with garlic, rosemary
    & bacon 142
mousse, Chocolate soufflé-cum-mousse 158, 159
muffins 60, 61, 62
mushrooms
    Barbecued, with anchovy mayonnaise 101
    Chicken & mushroom lasagne 147
    Creamed mushroom soup with soy 27
    Haggis-stuffed 155
    Mushroom, lemon & noodle soup 34, 35
    Mushroom pizza 96, 97

Mushroom risotto cakes 80
    Partridge with wild mushroom sauce 151
    Pasta with mushrooms 85
    Tuna, artichoke & mushroom cobbler 92
mussels
    Barbecued, in foil 110, 111
    Mussel & saffron crêpes 124
    Mussels with chilli & coriander 87

Nectarine & blueberry slump 177
noodles
    Beef with black bean sauce & noodles 88
    Chinese noodle salad with mango,
        crab & ginger 148, 149
    Hawker's spicy noodles 94, 95
    Mushroom, lemon & noodle soup 34, 35

Oatmeal pastry 132
omelettes
    Courgette & mint tortilla 101
    Ham & spinach 55
orange
    Duck & orange salad 46, 47
    Duck with orange-roasted radicchio 140
    Panettone French toast with orange-fried
        blueberries 57
Oregano cornbread 72
Oysters with guacamole 17

Pacific ceviche 22
pancakes
    Banana, with maple syrup 62
    Lamb & tomato crêpe stack 126, 127
    Mussel & saffron crêpes 124
Pancetta & fig salad with hazelnut dressing 41
Panettone French toast with orange-fried
    blueberries 57
papaya, Bacon, avocado & papaya salad 50, 51
Parma ham, Scrambled eggs with Parma ham 54
Parmesan snaps 138
parsnips
    Juniper gratin 141
    Parsnip soup with Arbroath smokies 31
    Roasted pumpkin soup 36
    Shepherd's pie with parsnip topping 125
    Smoked haddock & parsnip salad
        with roasted chilli vinaigrette 41
Partridge with wild mushroom sauce 151
pasta
    Chicken & mushroom lasagne 147
    Crab & dill 89
    Fresh tomato & feta penne 115
    Pasta with lemon & cream 14
    Pasta with mushrooms 85
    Pasta risotto 93
    see also noodles
pavlova, Chocolate macadamia 161
Peanut butter & jelly muffins 62
pears
    Banana, toffee & pear crumble 160
    Pear & cranberry tarte tatin 179
    Roasted, with sesame praline ice-cream 166
    Stilton & pear salad 20, 21
pecan nuts
    Marinated Brussels sprouts with pecans 154
    Sticky pecan brownies 186, 187
peppers
    Black bean & red pepper salad 44
    Granary picnic loaf with salami & grilled
        peppers 102, 103
    Roasted ratatouille vinaigrette 18, 19
    Roasted red pepper soup 26
    Sweet potato mash with yassa chicken 114
pesto, Sorrel 27
Pheasant breasts with mango sauce 139
Pheasant with gin 139
Plums in sloe gin 160
Poached eggs on pesto toast 70, 71
polenta
    Chocolate cake with fig & chocolate cream
        189
    Mincemeat polenta crumble bars 186, 188
    Polenta-fried tomatoes 58, 59
    Rabbit with green olives, figs & polenta 128
    see also cornmeal

pork
  Hawker's spicy noodles 94, *95*
  Hot pork & apple loaf *78*, 79
  Meatloaf with roasted hazelnut &
    tomato sauce 118
  Pork casserole with black pudding crust 121
  Roast, with cinnamon apples 144, *145*
potatoes
  Potato & herb bread 72
  Saffron mash 141
  Sauna sausage with new potato salad 67
  Steak & chips with Roquefort butter 89
prawns
  Gazpacho with prawns 28, *29*
  Luxury fish pie with prawns 122, *123*
  Prawn & mint salad 42
  Prawn, avocado & cheese quesadillas 79
  Prawns with coconut 66
  Prawns with lemongrass mayo 16
preserves 63, 105, *130*, 131
Provençal tuna & rice salad 50
puddings
  Black-cap 163
  Chocolate macadamia steamed *172*, *173*
  Crunchie 182
  Hot chocolate fudge 166
  Mexican bread & butter 174
pumpkin
  Pumpkin wedges 150
  Roasted pumpkin & sesame salad 40
  Roasted pumpkin soup 36

quesadillas, Prawn, avocado & cheese 79
quince
  Lamb & quince tagine 115
  Quince & vanilla compote 164
  Walnut & quince tart with quince cream 167

Rabbit with green olives, figs & polenta 128
radicchio, Duck with orange-roasted radicchio 140
raspberries
  Raspberry crumble cake 183
  Raspberry jam with Drambuie 63
  Warm berry compote with rose petal ice-
    cream 164, *165*
ratatouille, Roasted ratatouille vinaigrette *18*, 19
rhubarb, Warm rhubarb compote with white
  chocolate sorbet 171
rice & risotti
  Barley risotto 84
  Beetroot & red wine risotto 90, *91*
  Cheese-stuffed rice balls *137*, 138
  Mushroom risotto cakes 80
  Pasta risotto 93
  Provençal tuna & rice salad 50
Roast cod with a coconut & lime sauce & mango
  salsa 146
Roast fennel *152*, *153*
Roast grouse with blackcurrants 140
Roast monkfish with garlic, rosemary
  & bacon 142
Roast pork with cinnamon apples 144, *145*
Roasted chilli vinaigrette 41
Roasted garlic aïoli 143
Roasted hazelnut & tomato sauce 118
Roasted pears with sesame praline ice-cream 166
Roasted pumpkin & sesame salad 40
Roasted pumpkin soup 36
Roasted ratatouille vinaigrette *18*, 19
Roasted red pepper soup 26
rock cakes, Choc-chip toffee 184
rocket, Artichoke, rocket & Parmesan salad 40
Roquefort butter 89
Rose petal ice-cream 164, *165*
Rumbledethumps with haggis 155

Saffron & manchego tartlets 136, *137*
Saffron mash 141
salads
  Artichoke, rocket & Parmesan 40
  Bacon, avocado & papaya 50, *51*
  Black bean & red pepper 44
  Butter bean & parsley 44
  Caesar 47
  Duck & orange 46, *47*

Mint couscous tabbouleh 49
Pancetta & fig, with hazelnut dressing 41
Prawn & mint 42
Provençal tuna & rice 50
Roasted pumpkin & sesame 40
Roasted ratatouille vinaigrette *18*, 19
Sauna sausage with new potato salad 67
Scallop, with soy vinaigrette 42, *43*
Smoked haddock & parsnip, with
  roasted chilli vinaigrette 41
Steak 45
Stilton & pear 20, *21*
Thai seafood 48
salami, Granary picnic loaf with salami
  & grilled peppers 102, *103*
salmon
  Salmon & sorrel soup 27
  Salmon fillets with stir-fried cabbage
    & roasted garlic aïoli 143
  Salt- and dill-cured salmon 142
  smoked *see* smoked salmon
salsas *86*, *87*, *132*, 146
Salt- and dill-cured salmon 142
sauces
  Chocolate *162*, 163
  Coconut & lime 146
  Dipping 73
  Roasted hazelnut & tomato 118
  Tomato 84
  Tomato & basil 119
  Wild mushroom sauce 151
sausages
  Granary picnic loaf with salami &
    grilled peppers 102, *103*
  Sauna sausage with new potato salad 67
  Tortilla hot dogs 104
Scallop ceviche 12
Scallop salad with soy vinaigrette 42, *43*
scones, White pepper, with strawberries
  & clotted cream 184, *185*
Scrambled eggs with Parma ham 54
sea bass, Stuffed spicy 105
Shepherd's pie with parsnip topping 125
Sloe gin 160
Slow-braised lamb shanks *120*, 121
Slow-roasted tomatoes with Parmesan,
  olives & capers 17
slump, Nectarine & blueberry 177
smoked haddock
  Parsnip soup with Arbroath smokies 31
Smoked haddock & parsnip salad with
  roasted chilli vinaigrette 41
smoked salmon
  Bagels with lox & cream cheese 54
  Smoked salmon & cucumber sandwich loaf
    100
  Warm smoked salmon, Brie & avocado
    croissants 55
Smoked venison with melon 14, *15*
sorbet, White chocolate 171
Sorrel pesto 27
soufflés
  Chocolate soufflé-cum-mousse 158, *159*
Spinach & goat's cheese 13
soups 24-37
Spicy chicken kebabs 108
spinach
  Anchovy & spinach tart 68, *69*
  Calzone with Taleggio, garlic & spinach 76
  Chicken breasts with spinach, tomato &
    mozzarella 84
  Grenadian spinach & coconut soup 34
  Ham & spinach omelette 55
  Spinach & goat's cheese soufflé 13
  Spinach empanadas 104
squid
  Stir-fried, with lemongrass 12
  Stuffed, with lemon oil 133
steak
  Beef with black bean sauce & noodles 88
  Steak & chips with Roquefort butter 89
  Steak salad 45
  *see also* beef
Sticky pecan brownies *186*, 187
Stilton & pear salad 20, 21

Stir-fried squid with lemongrass 12
strawberries
  Strawberry, mint & chocolate brownie trifle
    176
  Warm berry compote with rose petal ice-
    cream 164, *165*
  White pepper scones with strawberries
    & clotted cream 184, *185*
Stuffed spicy sea bass 105
Stuffed squid with lemon oil 133
swede, Rumbledethumps with haggis 155
Swedish roast lamb with coffee & cream 154
sweet potatoes
  Grenadian spinach & coconut soup 34
  Sweet potato mash with yassa chicken 114

tabbouleh, Mint couscous tabbouleh 49
Tablet 111
tagine, Lamb & quince 115
Tarragon turkey 150
tarts & tartlets
  Anchovy & spinach 68, *69*
  Chicory & Gruyère 132
  Chocolate-crusted lemon 174, *175*
  Pear & cranberry tarte tatin 179
  Saffron & manchego 136, *137*
  Three-tomato 81
  Treacle 178
  Walnut & quince, with quince cream 167
Thai fish balls with dipping sauce 73
Thai seafood salad 48
Three-tomato tart 81
Thunder & lightning 173
Tom yam soup 31
tomatoes
  Baked tomato eggs 76
  Chicken breasts with spinach, tomato &
    mozzarella 84
  Chicken with pesto & tomato & basil sauce
    119
  Fresh tomato & feta penne 115
  Lamb & tomato crêpe stack 126, *127*
  Marinated tuna with roasted tomato
    relish 106, *107*
  Meatloaf with roasted hazelnut &
    tomato sauce 118
  Polenta-fried tomatoes 58, *59*
  Slow-roasted tomatoes with
    Parmesan, olives & capers 17
  Three-tomato tart 81
  Tomato & Marmite bruschetta 68
  Tomato & pesto clafoutis 94
tonnato, Turkey 151
Tortilla hot dogs 104
Treacle tart 178
trifle, Strawberry, mint & chocolate brownie 176
Trout with *chermoula* crust 88
tuna
  Marinated, with roasted tomato relish 106, *107*
  Provençal tuna & rice salad 50
  Tuna, artichoke & mushroom cobbler 92
turkey
  Tarragon 150
  Turkey tonnato 151
Turkish aubergine dip with garlic & dill 19

venison
  Smoked venison with melon 14, *15*
  Venison chilli 116, *117*

walnuts
  Chicken with a coriander & walnut
    crust & fried capers 90
  Walnut & quince tart with quince cream 167
  Walnut bread with goat's cheese 71
Warm berry compote with rose petal
  ice-cream 164, *165*
Warm date cake with coconut fudge topping 188
Warm rhubarb compote with white
  chocolate sorbet 171
Warm smoked salmon, Brie & avocado
  croissants 55
White chocolate sorbet 171
White pepper scones with strawberries
  & clotted cream 184, *185*